CHILDREN THROUGH THE AGES

Through the ages children were exploited, abandoned, sacrificed and, occasionally, romanticized and enjoyed. But most of the time they were ignored. When people did stop to think of children at all, they viewed them either as miniature adults or as peculiar, unformed animals. How we got from this negative idea of children to the near-adoration of them we find in America today is the subject of this book.

Beginning with early man, the author searches the past, bringing whole eras to life as she focuses in turn on childhood in the ancient world, the Middle Ages, and Renaissance, early modern times, the Victorian era and, in America, every century from the colonial period to the present.

Mrs. Greenleaf has drawn upon an enormous number of sources for her narrative, ranging from the Bible and Margaret Mead's anthropology to collections of old toys. Her evidence is startling. It shows how the years of childhood have stretched out and changed; how the child's status has risen from being his father's possession to being a person with rights under the law; and how, above all, we have grown in our understanding of what it means to be young.

BARBARA KAYE GREENLEAF

CHILDREN THROUGH THE AGES

A HISTORY OF CHILDHOOD

McGRAW-HILL BOOK COMPANY

NEW YORK · ST. LOUIS · SAN FRANCISCO · AUCKLAND ·
BOGOTÁ· DÜSSELDORF · JOHANNESBURG · LONDON · MADRID
· MEXICO · MONTREAL · NEW DELHI · PANAMA · PARIS · SÃO
PAULO · SINGAPORE · SYDNEY · TOKYO · TORONTO

Frontispiece—*Family Group,* sculpture by Henry Moore (1948–49). Bronze (cast 1950), 59¼ × 46½, at base, 45 × 29⅞. Collection, The Museum of Modern Art, New York. A. Conger Goodyear Fund.

Library of Congress Cataloging in Publication Data

Greenleaf, Barbara Kaye.
    Children through the ages.

    Bibliography: p.
    Includes index.
    SUMMARY: A history of childhood from earliest times to today focusing on infancy, the middle years, and adolescence and discussing toys, games, food, diseases, discipline, clothing, health care, and education.
    1. Children—History—Juvenile literature.
[1. Children—History] I. Title.
HQ781.G67   301.43′14   77-78758
ISBN 0-07-024355-7

1234567890 BPBP 783210987

For Jon, Carrie, and Cathy

CONTENTS

ACKNOWLEDGMENTS

I would like to thank my typists Patricia McClain and Suzanne Hill and the many librarians who assisted me in this vast research project. But above all I would like to thank my colleague Dr. Lewis A. Schaffer, who contributed professional knowledge to the sections on pediatrics and psychological insights to the work as a whole. *CHILDREN THROUGH THE AGES* is a stronger book for his help.

The father then lifted the baby in the air above his head and kissed it on the thigh, calling out "My Cattle," for that was what it represented to his imagination.

—Dudley Kidd, *The Essential Kaffir, 1904*.

CHILDHOOD: NOW AND THEN

Americans are a people obsessed with child-rearing. In their books, magazines, talk shows, parent training courses, White House conferences, and chats over the back fence, they endlessly debate the best ways to raise children. Moreover, Americans do more than debate their theories; they translate them into action. They erect playgrounds for the youngsters' pleasure, equip large schools for their education, and train skilled specialists for their welfare. Whole industries in America are devoted to making children happy, healthy, and wise.

But this interest in childhood is relatively new. In fact, until very recently people considered childhood just a brief, unimportant prelude to adulthood and the real business of living. By and large they either ignored children, beat them, or fondled them carelessly, much as we would amuse ourselves with a litter of puppies. When they gave serious thought to children at all, people either conceived of them as miniature adults or as peculiar, unformed animals. The prevailing attitude was summed up by the French essayist Montaigne, who declared that children had "neither mental activities nor recognizable bodily shape."

How we got from this negative view of young people to the near-adoration of them we find in America today is the subject of this book. But before we begin our inquiry, let us first define childhood. Quite simply it is the absence of adulthood. Adults can earn their own living, set up their own household, reproduce children and enjoy all the privileges that go with being a full-fledged member of society. Children cannot do these things. At some point they will be able to, but that point has fluctuated from as young as eight to as old as thirty, depending on the standards of the group.

Down through the ages the experiences of childhood have been as varied as its duration. Actions that would have provoked a beating in one era elicit extra loving care in another. Babies who would have been nurtured exclusively by their mothers in one epoch are left with day-care workers in another. In some places children have been trained to straddle unsteady canoes, negotiate treacherous mountain passes, and carry heavy bundles on their heads. In other places they have been taught complicated piano concerti and long multiplication tables.

But diverse as it has been, childhood has one common experience at its core and that is the social aspect of nurture. All children need adults to bring them up. Because human young take so long to become independent, we think that civilization may have grown up around the need to feed and protect them. Certainly, from the earliest days of man, adults have made provision for the children in their midst.

CHAPTER ONE

EARLY MAN

At one breathless moment in history some apes began to walk upright and never went down on all fours again. We don't know when that time was or when they became recognizable as men, but gradually they developed an intelligence and dexterity that surpassed any of God's other creatures. These pre-men were rather small by our standards, yet some two million years ago, as *Homo habilis,* they began to hunt large animals. With that momentous step their commitment to food sharing, group hunting, and other aspects of social life greatly increased.

But for many centuries before they went after big game, the first recognizable people were principally gatherers who lived on the nuts, berries, and grasses that grew all around them. As long as gathering was the main way of life, even very small children could make an important contribution. Mother, father, and offspring probably all foraged together and shared the work equally back at the home base, too. However, once hunting became a major factor, the family may have begun to divide up the work. Nursing women and small children would have slowed the hunters' pace, so they may have continued to forage around home while the men went out after large animals. Although we cannot be sure of this pattern, it seems logical, judging from the behavior of the most primitive societies in the world today.

Since very young children were a drain on their parents, one wonders why prehistoric man nurtured them. Did he do it solely on instinct? Out of some innate tenderness? From a desire to perpetuate the group? Perhaps the answer is a mixture of all three, just as it is today. Early man seemed to feel an overriding allegiance to the group which ensured his food and safety. Since only numbers would keep the group strong, he needed to have offspring. Indeed, prehistoric man seemed to be overwhelmingly absorbed with the propagation of his own species as well as with that of every living thing on which he depended. In his longing for fertility, he made the pregnant woman the embodiment of his most fevent hopes. She appears time and again in prehistoric representations, her belly great and round with child.

Once he got them, early man probably treated his children well. We infer this from his seeming fondness for all dependent creatures, a fondness which led him to make pets of wild birds and animals by throwing them food. We also infer it from the generally good care given the young in the most primitive societies today. This is especially true where food is abundant and life can be relaxed and amiable. Anthropologists have found that the !Kung Bushmen of the Kalahari Desert and other primitive hunter-gatherers work less and enjoy more leisure than do most farmers today. And they are very attentive to their children, too. Prehistoric man probably paid his off-spring the same attention, because many experts feel that at the dawn of human history the environment was kind.

They also feel that life was short. From the skeletons and skulls of *Australopithecus* men, who were erect but still had the cranial capacity of apes, scientists have concluded that most of them didn't live to be twenty. Since *Australopithecus* had a childhood at least as long as that of chimpanzees, a great many of them must have been orphaned. Yet they survived and multiplied, so we can infer that the group provided for them in some fashion and gave them the education they needed to survive. Indeed, adoption must be part of our social-genetic makeup, because observers have noted it so frequently among primitive peoples.

In prehistoric times children probably had few friends their own age, because where survival depends on hunting and gathering, only a very few people can be supported in any given territory. Australian aborigines, for example, rarely live in groups of more than fifty and more usually their number is limited to the members of a single family. The traditional Eskimo society is limited to groups of ten or twenty families, and these rarely add up to more than one hundred individuals in all. Prehistoric peoples, like many primitive peoples, must have known about their neighbors and had some sort of contact with them, but each probably remained essentially within its own well-defined territory—a territory chronically short of age-mates.

Children would have had a hard time maintaining friendships in any case, because they were frequently on the move. Although a home is usually equated with a fixed, settled family life in the folk tales of the world, "home" was probably a very transitory affair in prehistoric times. It might have meant no more than a brief encampment at the mouth of a cave or the construction of a flimsy windbreak. Even today among many of the most primitive peoples—the Australian aborigine, the African Bushman and some South American Indians—home often consists of just a few hastily erected sticks covered with grasses which suffices for a night or two. For them as for prehistoric man, the total environment is the true home.

Children shared the home environment with their parents in prehistoric times, just as they share a split-level house with them today. But thousands of years ago they also shared the adults' life to an extent unknown to civilized man. Being so dependent on the environment, parents could not shield their offspring from hardships even if they had wanted to. When times were good, both parents and children feasted; when times were hard all of them starved. Moreover, parents had no special knowledge which divided them from the youngsters. As civilization progressed there might be one called "shaman," who knew of special magical cures, or perhaps one strong one who became known as "chief." Otherwise, everyone did the same work and one member of the group, no matter what his age, was probably like every other member.

Yet children may have played a unique role in the development of civilization, for man's first rules seem to have concerned the young: who shall rear them, to whom they shall belong, with whom they may have sexual relations, and whom they may marry. Throughout the world the welfare of children seems to be at the heart of all social structure. Indeed, anthropologist Bronislaw Malinowski has come to the conclusion that marriage was introduced not to sanction sexual relations or to establish a framework for monogamy, but rather to provide for the production and maintenance of children. And in their *History of Pediatrics* Isaac Abt and Fielding H. Garrison claim that the religious and legal sanctions of marriage still exist essentially for the benefit of children. The fact that marriage makes the union of a man and woman respectable is incidental in their view.

There is evidence, too, that the nuclear family is central to the development of civilization. A grouping of three large figures dating back to the neolithic period some seven thousand years ago has been unearthed in Jericho, Israel, one of the wellsprings of civilization. Presumably a shrine, these three figures represent a man, woman, and child—the sacred family trinity that has recurred so often in the religion, folklore, and art of the world. Indeed, the nuclear family has been one of the most universal and tenacious ideas in all of human experience. Even in societies where more than one woman mothers a child or an uncle or grandfather assumes the role of father, we can recognize the basic family unit, because it is so much like our own.

As the millennia passed, the species *Homo sapiens* evolved and fanned out around the globe. We shall follow his progress in the Western world, because it is from that branch of civilization that our own culture has developed. To set the stage for a discussion of the child in modern times, let us look first at his lot in ancient times. We shall do so in four of the most important cultures of the era: Egypt, Israel, Greece, and Rome.

CHAPTER TWO

HONOR THY FATHER AND MOTHER

Many thousands of years ago in the warm, fertile lands between the Tigris and Euphrates rivers and along the Nile Valley, men began to come together in large numbers. Over time they stopped trying to gather, grow, or hunt everything their families needed and started developing skills and wares instead. They bartered these specialties for the things they didn't have and couldn't make or grow.

In order to perform the new, specialized tasks of civilization, a person needed more training than ever before. He got much of that training in childhood, which came to be thought of as the time of education. Over the millennia the definition of education was expanded until upper-class families felt they had to direct every aspect of their youngsters' moral, physical, and intellectual development. As a result life grew complicated for many children, but it grew even more complicated for their parents. With the development of civilization, nurturing took on emotional overtones it had probably never had before. Hope and fear, joy and disappointment started to color parental feelings from the moment the baby was born.

"A BLESSING HAS COME INTO THE WORLD"

Lo, children are an heritage of the Lord; and the fruit of the womb is his reward.

—Psalms, 127:3

The first order God gave man was "Be fruitful and multiply," and Hebrew religious leaders, called rabbis, took this injunction so seriously that some even said "a childless man should be thought of as dead." Children were crucial to that small, struggling band of Israelites, because only they could perpetuate the tribe. Though the Hebrews called every child a gift of God, in fact they did not greet all newborns with equal rejoicing. They were happiest about the first son, because he would be head of the household one day.

Firstborn or not, a boy was always preferable to a girl as far as the Israelites or other ancient (and most modern) peoples were concerned. When a boy was born, the Hebrews said "a blessing has come into the world," but when a girl was born everyone agreed that "the walls wept." A boy would contribute to the family, whereas a girl would take away from it in the form of a dowry. Moreover, after marriage she would belong to her husband's family. As the Talmud stated: "Girls are but an illusory treasure; besides, they have to be watched continually."

Many ancient peoples wanted to ensure that the newborn, girl or boy, adhered to their standards of beauty. The Egyptians admired an elongated or cone-shaped head and they used a variety of contraptions to compress the infant's head into the desired shape. The Greeks preferred a well-rounded shape, which the midwives tried to assure by modeling the newborn's head with their hands, a process that is carried on in parts of Greece to this day. They also restrained or manipulated his arms, legs, and spine for the sake of beauty, and the great medical writer Soranus of Ephesus even wrote out a prescription for the production of a good-looking navel. Instead of tying the umbilical cord to the thigh as was the common custom, he recommended that it be "placed gently in the middle of the umbilical area, to result in a well-defined hollow."

Although much about infant care must have remained the same since prehistoric times, the coming of civilization did introduce one important difference. Now upper-class women could hand over the chore of nursing to servants or slaves, thereby retaining their freedom and their shape. This practice of using wet nurses was never condoned by philosophers and moralists. The Hebrew prophets sternly warned mothers that it was their duty to nurse and Plutarch tried to convince women of its emotional benefits, declaring "this fellowship in feeding is a bond that knits kindliness together." But their words seem to have fallen on deaf ears. According to the Roman writer Tacitus, "Today, as soon as he is born, the child is abandoned to any old Greek servant, who has been assigned one or two slaves chosen in a haphazard way. . . ." And Aulus Gellius said tersely, "They take the first woman who has milk."

Since the use of wet nurses was so widespread, advice givers spent a great deal of time discussing their selection and deportment. Down through the centuries the same points were continually stressed: the wet nurse was not to drink too much wine, eat highly spiced foods, or sleep with a man. The most important thing about her, though, was that she had to have good milk. In the second century A.D., Soranus proposed his famous fingernail test for breast milk which remained the rule of thumb for seventeen hundred years:

> Whether the milk will coagulate properly is determined by the fact that if we put a drop on the fingernail or on a laurel leaf or other smooth surface it slowly spreads and when shaken, retains the drop-form; for if it flows at once in all directions, it is watery, but if it coheres like honey and does not change its drop-form, it is too thick.

TOYS, TUNICS, TABLE MANNERS

Among the gifts received by an Athenian baby there was usually a rattle or two. This age-old cradle toy was fashioned in many materials and shapes and the Greek infant was likely to clutch a fat clay pig in his fist before he was too many days old. In the succeeding months and years the child received many other playthings, some of them homemade, others products of a thriving toy industry. Because the Greeks admired physical prowess, many of their toys and games helped develop their youngsters' bodies. Small Greek children played on a kind of teeter-board which promoted balance, for example, while older boys rolled the hoop, as much to keep in shape as for fun. Greek girls improved their manual dexterity with knuckle-bones, a game akin to our jacks, and developed grace through dancing. Egyptians, too, may have been interested in physical fitness, because, in addition to depicting variations of snatch-the-club and piggyback rides, their wall paintings show children in poses remarkably similar to our calisthenics.

Throughout the ancient world children engaged in play imitations of the adult world. In warlike Greece and Rome, boys enjoyed maneuvering toy soldiers, chariots, and miniature war machines. Egyptian boys of the warrior class also enjoyed martial activities. They staged mock battles with small versions of the axes, slings, and bows and arrows that their fathers used in real combat. In Greece men often went off to war in ships and children treasured small replicas of their boats. One of these replicas, made seven hundred years before the birth of Christ, can still be seen in the British Museum. It is a Corinthian warship manned by five warriors with shields. Not all the toys and games had to do with war, however, for the Bible speaks of Hebrew children imitating adults in games of "feast" and "burial." Elsewhere in the ancient world there were working models of shops and factories and tiny imitations of real-life cups, plates, beds, and other household furnishings. While some of these miniatures may have been intended for religious purposes—indeed, our word "doll" comes from the Greek word for "idol"—many of them must have been used for play. At least this is the assumption of one authority on the subject, Antonia Fraser, who points out that the tiny Roman furniture on display in the British Museum is on a scale of one inch to one foot, the same scale we use in our dollhouses.

Some toys and games which were favorites with children in

the ancient world are favorites with children today, too. Balls, tops, and kites are examples of these durable pastimes as are hobbyhorses and riddles. Push and pull-along toys were also standard nursery equipment then as now. Theirs were made of wood, clay, and stone while ours are made of plastic, but the designs bear a remarkable resemblance to one another. Many of the ancient toys were realistic replicas of the domestic animals that were familiar to every small child. But some of the surviving playthings displayed in European museums, such as the blue mouse with brown spots, the crocodile with movable jaw and the ape driving a chariot, show that they could also be whimsical or exotic. Children enjoyed real animals as well as replicas and they had a variety of household pets to choose from. The Egyptians thought that cats had a particular affinity for children. If a royal child died, a favorite cat might be mummified and placed in the young boy's or girl's tomb to provide companionship on the journey to the Kingdom of the Dead.

Throughout the ages little girls have enjoyed playing with dolls, and those children who lived in ancient times were no exception. Upper-class Egyptian girls played with dolls made of wood, clay, or rags stuffed with straw. Some of their "babies" had beaded hair, some were brightly painted, and some had jointed arms and legs. In ancient times dolls were often fitted out with clothes and, in the case of one surviving Roman figure, gold bangle arm bracelets and a ring. Dolls provided hours of diversion to which their young owners responded with love and heartfelt concern. The Greek biographer Plutarch noted that his two-year-old daughter, Timoxena, even begged the wet nurse to suckle her doll as well as herself.

Egyptians, who treasured their toys as mementos of childhood, put them into storage as they grew up but did not discard them. Greek and Roman children did not throw away their playthings, either. When they reached puberty they consecrated them to the gods above, as testified to by a memorial tablet at the altar of the goddess of love. "O Aphrodite, despise not my doll's purple neckerchief," it states; "I, Sappho, dedicate this precious gift to you."

Young children could move about freely in their play, because their clothes were either very simple or nonexistent. Little girls at the Egyptian royal court generally went naked until the age of five or more. Like their mothers, though, they wore heavy black eye makeup, splendid beaded necklaces, and, for public functions, long white garments. Other girls in the ancient world also wore a great deal of jewelry. Babylonian girls wore heavy half-moon pendants and earrings and little Hebrew girls wore nose rings, which they removed for the Sabbath to allow them to greet others without interference. Egyptian girls placed wigs over their shaven heads when they went out in public and Greek girls sometimes pulled their hair back into ponytails. Greek and Roman girls wore flowing tunic dresses and gaily colored cloaks of linen or wool while their brothers wore simple kilts, tunics, or, for great occasions, togas.

Children and adults in the ancient world ate with their fingers, as do many peoples today, and they were permitted to lick them with propriety. But that doesn't mean that there was no such thing as table manners. Thousands of years before the birth of Christ Egyptian youngsters were admonished:

> When thou art seated among the guests of a great man, accept what he giveth thee gracefully. Look before thee, nor stare at the food, nor look at it often; he that departest from this rule is a boorish fellow.

THE THINKING SHOPS

In ancient times childhood was always brief among the lower classes. It consisted of a few fleeting years of play before the youngsters had to join their parents in the fields. It was none too long for girls of the upper classes, either, for they began their training in the domestic arts at an early age. A few females were taught their ABCs and a few were educated beyond that, but they were the exceptions. In the ancient world education was almost exclusively reserved for boys, and upper-class boys at that.

These privileged males began their education at varying times. Jewish boys started school at the age of five and Greek boys began at seven, but some philosophers worried about the time lost before that. Plato would have had youngsters begin their education at age six, Aristotle said five and Chrysippus thought even three was not too early to enter school.

Classrooms in the ancient world were not elaborate. In Rome the primary school building was a simple, shedlike affair attached to a public building. It had a roof but its sides were open, so the children were constantly being distracted by street traffic. Greek and Roman children learned to write by scratching on a wax tablet with the pointed end of a stylus or stick. Roman children learned their alphabet from letters cut out of ivory and Egyptian children learned arithmetic by dividing up fruit. In Greece boys studied from scrolls as much as twelve feet long. Since they had no desks, the children had to wind and unwind these ungainly papyrus bundles across their knees, which was no mean feat.

The schooling they received varied from culture to culture. In Egypt, for example, education was really vocational training. Any boy who became a "writer in the house of books" was expected to come out of it as a priest, scribe, doctor, soldier, musician, or artisan. Egyptian boys practiced their writing by copying out the sayings of their wise men. "Be diligent at all times," "Do more than is commanded," and "Waste not the time wherein thou canst labour" are typical of the puritanical commands they had to write out. These assignments were intended to develop moralistic attitudes as well as a fine hand.

Encouraging good behavior was also an integral part of Greek education. Greek boys had to memorize long passages about the siege of Troy and the adventures of Odysseus, on the theory that they would want to emulate the strong moral fiber of the epics' heroes. But in some cases they enjoyed the gory battle scenes so much that they may have missed the moral point altogether. Greek boys also studied rhetoric, philosophy, mathematics, and music. Music played a large part in Athenian life—some of the laws were even set to music—and philosophers were particularly eager for boys to learn it. They believed that if harmony and rhythm entered boys' souls, it would make them gentler and more refined. Upper-class boys learned to play the lyre and, to a lesser extent, the flute, although some adults considered flute music too exciting for a boy's own good.

Since the Greeks admired the all-around man, their sons were likely to spend as much time perfecting javelin throws and wrestling holds as studying philosophy and the sciences. After school the boys went to the Academy, the great sports center of the Greek city-state Athens, where they proceeded to strip off all their clothes and rub their naked bodies with oil to make the limbs supple. Then they took lessons in riding, running, jumping, wrestling, and swimming. Roman boys went through the same paces at the Campus Martius and the Tiber, but they exercised to make the body hard, whereas the Greeks were more interested in making it beautiful.

Over the centuries the acquisition of knowledge became more important to the Greeks than prowess in sports. But not everyone was in favor of this trend. Old-timers spoke out against the long hours spent in the "thinking shops," which they said produced bookworms with "pale faces, small shoulders, narrow chests, and long tongues." They preferred the old days when hard work in the gymnasium produced healthy bodies and good, stolid, unquestioning boys who didn't think they knew more than their fathers. But even when the Greeks upgraded book learning, they never completely dropped their attention to physical development. Both they and the Romans thought of intellectual and physical development as complementary processes. The Latin phrase *mens sana in corpore sano,* "a sound mind in a sound body," sums up the ideal for both civilizations.

To the warlike Spartans, inhabitants of another Greek city-state, the only thing that counted in life was toughness in battle. Since even talking was considered a sign of weakness—the best Spartans communicated through a series of grunts—it is not surprising that their children spent little time on formal education beyond the rudiments of reading and writing. "School" really consisted of military training. Spartan boys were taught how to forage for food in a barren countryside, how to handle a sword and spear, and how to form a shield wall in battle. Their training games were vicious free-for-alls in which boys could kick, bite, and even gouge out the opponents' eyes in order to drive them into the river and win the game. Girls in Sparta were also brought up to be tough. One day they would be expected to produce many babies just like other women in the ancient world, but as children they were taught gymnastics and sports like their brothers.

The ancient Hebrews were poles apart from the Spartans on the subject of education. To them it was critical. Indeed, one of the rabbis' favorite maxims was: "If you have knowledge, you have everything; if you do not possess knowledge, you possess nothing." Since the Israelites' culture and religion were one and the same, they learned all their lessons—the alphabet, vocabulary, grammar, history, and geography—from their holy book, the Torah. The Hebrews said that "a child ought to be fattened with the Torah as an ox is fattened in the stall."

Whereas among other peoples only wealthy boys could afford to go to school, which was always private in the ancient world, the Hebrews saw to it that all their boys, rich or poor, could attend the *beth sefer,* or "house of the book." In fact, some sixty years before the birth of Jesus, the high priest Joshua ben Gamala put forth what may be the world's first piece of educational legislation. He made education mandatory and even threatened to punish children who played hooky.

Because of education's central role in Jewish life, the rabbis, who were both scholars and teachers, occupied positions of leadership. Even those men who taught young children were held in high regard, as befitted people who imparted God's word. The Jews called a teacher "the messenger of the Almighty," and the Talmud said, "A teacher should be venerated as much as God himself." In Egypt scribes and teachers, often one and the same, were also among the most respected and learned members of the community.

But the situation was vastly different in the rest of the ancient world. In Greece and Rome teachers commanded little respect and less money. They were often slaves or reputable men who had come down on their luck and had turned to teaching as a last resort. Indeed, it was said of someone who was missing that "he's either dead or else he's teaching somewhere." Anyone could set himself up as a master because there were no requirements for the job and only one known way of doing it—sheer repetition. The Hebrews said that the maxims of God's laws said over and over again "go in by the blood and come out at the lips."

In ancient times children lost interest in their lessons no less than they do today. Greek vase paintings often show students playing with their dogs or pet cheetahs instead of paying attention to the master, and nearby dwellers complained that schools made noisy neighbors. Angered by the disorder, masters raised their voices and then, more often than not, retaliated with brutal corporal punishment. But beatings were an accepted practice in the ancient world, where the motto of Greek schools was "No progress without painful effort" and the Hebrew word *musar* meant both education and chastisement. As Proverbs summed up the prevailing attitude: "Boyhood's mind is loaded with a pack of folly, that needs the rod of correction to shift it."

"TODAY YOU ARE A MAN"

Between the ages of sixteen and eighteen, upper-class Greek and Roman boys bridged the gap between childhood and adulthood and became men. For the Greeks this meant serving in the army, for the Romans it meant serving in the government. For the Jewish boys who came of age at thirteen, it meant serving God.

The Israelites marked this great day in a boy's life with a religious ceremony called the *Bar Mitzvah,* or "Son of the Commandment." In the course of the ceremony the rabbi blessed the boy and told him, in effect, "Today you are a man." From that day on he would be expected to pray three times a day and fast on the designated holidays like all the other adult Jewish males. Moreover, before this time he was said to have sinned on his father's account, whereas now he sinned on his own account.

While the Bar Mitzvah was a puberty rite, it was also a graduation from school. By and large it marked the conclusion of a Jewish boy's education and the start of his working life, usually as an apprentice to his father. The Bar Mitzvah also marked the age at which a boy could marry, but few probably wed that young. Some rabbis felt that eighteen was considered the ideal age for matrimony, while a father "still had his hand upon his [son's] neck." The Israelites put a great deal of pressure on a boy to marry, because the family was the basis of their culture, a religious entity unto itself. To them an unmarried man would always be a boy, or as one rabbi put it, "A bachelor is not truly a man at all."

Girls had no choice in the matter: they had to marry. But though marriage spelled the end of childhood for them, it did not mean the beginning of independence. Girls married very young in every ancient society, usually before their fifteenth birthday, and they often became pregnant soon after. It has been estimated that Mary was no more than fourteen when she

bore Jesus, for example. For the most part these girls were simple and uneducated and had rarely strayed beyond the confines of their parents' homes. They would not start doing so now that they had homes of their own. In Babylonia some women managed their own estates and in Egypt some ladies of rank owned property, ran businesses, and acted as scribes in the courts of law. But these were the exceptions. Almost every girl in the ancient world merely substituted her husband's authority for her father's and, though married, she continued to have the status of a child.

But marriage did not always mean complete independence for men either. In Sparta a soldier was allowed to marry at the age of twenty, but he had to live in the army barracks until the age of thirty. Only then could he truly establish his own home. At thirty, too, he was accorded the full rights of a Spartan citizen, but it was understood that the state would continue to be his "parent" and that his first allegiance had to be to that parent rather than to his own family.

In Rome full independence often came very late, too, because all members of the family line, male or female, married or single, child or adult, were subject to the will of the oldest male member of the family line, the *paterfamilias*. They could not marry without his consent or own anything of their own, and any money they borrowed was charged to him. The pater-familias continued to hold this power over his relations not until they "grew up" but until the day *he* died. This absolute and perpetual dominion was found nowhere in the Western world except in Rome.

"IF IT IS A MALE, LET IT BE, IF A FEMALE EXPOSE IT"

During the thousands of years it took men to emerge from their wild state, they offered up their children to the gods. They slaughtered them on sacred altars as a way of making amends for past sins and a means of soliciting future favors. Child sacrifice stemmed from the supposition that the gods liked human food, especially the food of children who had just come from the other world. Since the firstborn son represented the greatest loss, he was often the one chosen to be killed. But many other children were taken also, as Plutarch notes in his description of the practice in Carthage:

> . . . With full knowledge and understanding they themselves offered up their own children and those who had no children would buy little ones from poor people and cut their throats as if they were so many lambs or young birds; meanwhile the mother stood by without a tear or moan; but should she utter a single moan or let fall a single tear, she had to forfeit the money, and her child was sacrificed nevertheless; and the whole area before the statue was filled with a loud noise of flutes and drums so that the cries of wailing should not reach the ears of the people.

Child sacrifice was widely practiced by the Phoenicians, Moabites, Ammonites, and many other ancient peoples. They did away with children for a variety of reasons in addition to propitiating the gods. In fact, infanticide was an accepted, everyday occurrence to the ancients, for whom it was the one sure means of population control. They practiced infanticide to prevent their estates from being split up among several sons, who would need expensive educations besides. First sons were allowed to live, but the boys who followed after were often not so fortunate. Infanticide was practiced in Sparta, where every citizen was a soldier and that soldier had to be the finest in the world. Weaklings could not be tolerated, so any child who seemed at all defective at birth was left outside to die. The ancients did away with children who were imperfect in size or shape, cried too much or too little, or were otherwise less than the ideal described in such gynecological writings as ''How to Recognize the Newborn That Is Worth Rearing.''

If not enslaved, illegitimate children, too, were often exposed. But the most likely candidate of all for exposure was the girl. Why go to the trouble of raising her, the ancients reasoned, when she would require a dowry and belong to her husband's family after marriage? Thus, in the first century B.C. an Egyptian husband named Illarion wrote home to his pregnant wife, Allis: "When you bear offspring, if it is a male let it be, if a female expose it."

The decision to let the baby live or die was made shortly after its birth, usually by the father or the paterfamilias. The newborn was laid at the man's feet and, if he picked the child up, it was allowed to live. If he turned away from it, a slave was dispatched to carry the infant from the house and get rid of it. The methods chosen varied from throwing babies into rivers to flinging them into dung heaps and "potting" them in jars. According to the Greek dramatist Euripedes, infants were exposed on every hill and roadside, "a prey for birds, food for wild beasts to rend."

Greek babies were often left with amulets or objects of some value to encourage their adoption. But "adoption" was not always to be preferred to death in ancient times, because the adopter often mutilated the children and made them into beggars who excited laughter and pity by their grotesque shapes. In his "Controversy" the Roman philosopher Seneca defends this common, if bizarre, practice:

> Look on the blind wandering about the streets leaning on their sticks, and those with crushed feet, and still again look on those with broken limbs. This one is without arms, that one has had its shoulders pulled down out of shape in order that his grotesqueries may excite laughter. . . . Let us go to the origin of all those ills—a laboratory for the manufacture of human wrecks—a cavern filled with the limbs torn from living children. . . . What wrong has been done to the Republic? On the contrary, have not these children been done a service inasmuch as their parents had cast them out?

It is hard for us to comprehend how these humanists could laugh at a mutilated child or how they could be entertained by the tale of a starving, dying infant. The Greeks could laugh, apparently, because they saw nothing wrong with infanticide. Both they and the Romans took it for granted that parents had the right to reject their own offspring, whereas the offspring, whose life was at stake, had no rights at all.

The Israelites never practiced infanticide for population control and early on in their history they rejected it for religious purposes, as well. Referring to an era one thousand years earlier, the writers of the Bible tell how the Lord commanded Abraham to sacrifice his firstborn son, Isaac, as a test of Abraham's devotion to Him. But when God saw that Abraham would follow through on his vow to kill his beloved son, He caused a ram to appear in Isaac's stead. This, the first recorded instance of an animal being substituted for a human life, was surely a great step forward for mankind. Later, the concept of ethical behavior accompanied and eventually replaced the practice of animal sacrifice.

Christianity carried on the humanitarian tradition of the Jewish religion from which it had sprung. Since one of Christianity's strongest beliefs was that every human being has a soul, the Church fathers condemned infanticide as a murderous act. As Barnabas articulated their stand: "Thou shalt not slay the child by procuring abortion, nor again shall thou destroy it after it is born." The early Christians apparently adhered to this position, because one contemporary was moved to remark on the respect they showed for the life of a child "even if it were newborn."

But the Jews and early Christians comprised just a tiny minority of the ancient world, and infanticide continued without letup. As a result there was a large imbalance of boys over girls, according to one authority, households were small—a boy and a girl were considered a large family in Greece—and the Roman upper class dwindled to the point of near-extinction. Then, shortly before the birth of Christ, the Emperor Augustus passed laws to make childrearing more palatable. He decreed that fathers were to be given tax relief, new social status, and preference for public office. But, according to Tacitus, "marriages and the rearing of children did not become more frequent, so powerful are the attractions of the childless state."

"WHAT WAS THE PURPOSE, CHILDREN, FOR WHICH I REARED YOU?"

The eye that mocketh at his father, and despiseth to obey his mother, the ravens of the valley shall pick it out, and the young eagles shall eat it.

—Proverbs, 30:17

The people of the ancient world seemed to have had as many conflicting emotions about their children as we do today. On the one hand they could coolly do away with their offspring through infanticide and child sacrifice; on the other hand they could show great concern for their welfare. In the Bible David grieved over his sick baby, and in the saga of Troy both Andromache and Hector mourned the death of their son. Moreover, if parents had not cared about their offspring, there would have been no point to Solomon's threat to cut a child in half to determine which of two disputing women was his real mother. The Greek philosopher Democritus summed up the ambiguity inherent in parenting: "To raise children is an uncertain thing. Success is attained only after a life of battle and disquietude. Their loss is followed by a sorrow which remains above all others."

The spirits of the ancient world reveal the mixed emotions with which parents viewed their offspring. In response to a very great and reasonable fear of the newborn being swept away by death, the Egyptians evolved two special gods to protect him: Maskonit, who appeared at the child's cradle at the moment of its birth, and Rainit, who gave him his name and saw to it that he was properly nursed. There were other helpful

Egyptian goddesses, too, who prevented the baby from being attacked by crocodiles, serpents, or dogs. In Greece, the goddess Hera looked out for small children and in Rome Juno performed the same function.

On the other side of the coin there were many spirits who intentionally harmed children. Semitic mythology had Lilith, a female demon who attacked youngsters in deserted places, and classical mythology had winged, brass-hoofed monsters who ate children or turned them into stone. The Greeks also dreamed up the *lamiae,* which are commonly represented with the head and breast of a woman and the body of a serpent. These fabulous monsters were supposed to allure young people in order to suck their blood.

Adults saw to it that children were well aware of the monsters who were out to get them, because frightening children was considered amusing. Children today enjoy a delicious fear of monsters, of course, but in ancient times the creatures were made out to be so horrible that they evoked nothing but stark terror. Adults also employed demons to keep the youngsters from talking to strangers or running away, much as parents recount lurid tales of child-stealing gypsies today.

Monster stories proved useful in day-to-day discipline as well. According to Dio Chrysostom, "terrifying images deter children when they want food or play or anything else unseasonable." And, he added, "I believe each youngster fears some bogy particular to himself and is wont to be terrified by this—of course, lads who are naturally timid cry out no matter what you produce to scare them. . . ."

As children grew older, adults found other ways of keeping them in line. They relied upon example, keeping their children close by them as they went about their duties. They also relied upon repetition: "Don't talk too loudly," "Don't sing in the public baths," "Don't walk too fast," "Don't sit with your cloak above your knees"—all these a Greek boy heard until he could recite them in his sleep. And they relied upon education.

But most of all the ancients relied upon harsh corporal punishment. As it was written in Proverbs: "Spare the rod, and thou art no friend to thy son."

From the repeated references to it, obedience seems to have been nothing short of an obsession in ancient times. As far back as the Egyptian's *Precepts of Ptha-Hotep,* perhaps the oldest book in the world, they hammered home the message of filial obedience. The Egyptian injunctions, "Bring up your son in obedience" and "Beloved of God is obedience; disobedience is hated by God" are remarkably similar to the biblical commandment, "Honor your father and your mother, that you may long endure on the land which the Lord your God is giving you." Like other ancient peoples the Israelites prescribed the death penalty for severe offenses against parents, although there is some doubt that they ever used it. The threat remained, however, as did the absolute rule of a father over his children.

Deference was owed to anyone above oneself in the ancient world. As the Egyptian scribe Ani advised his son, "Sit not while another standeth if he be older than thou or if he be your superior." And the Bible ordered, "Likewise, ye younger, submit yourselves unto the elder." But even more than deference was required for parents. They deserved honor. The rabbis commented endlessly on this point. In one of their typical stories illustrating filial piety a father strikes his son with a sandal in a moment of anger. When the sandal flies out of the father's hand, the boy retrieves it and gives it back, kissing the hand that has just struck him.

Why were the ancients so concerned with producing obedient offspring? Perhaps it stemmed from the perception of the child as something akin to the animals, something that had to be trained before it became human at all. Indeed, the ancients had few good things to say about children. The Greeks criticized their low level of artistic taste and their inability to reason clearly. In his *Historia Animalium* Aristotle compared their bodies to those of dwarfs. Like dwarfs, he said, they have weak memories because their heads weigh so much in relation to the rest of their bodies.

Beyond such disparaging remarks, the ancients said little about children. We know that they had some idea of the developmental process, because the Egyptians had separate hieroglyphs for "newborn" and "baby" and the Greeks and Romans had special names for young children, older children, and adolescents. Though they were great intuitive psychologists in other respects, they did not go beyond these crude divisions where children were concerned. They had no interest in the mysterious inner workings of childhood, because maturity was everything to them. All else was mere prelude. As St. Paul declared: "When I was a child, I spake as a child, I understood as a child, I thought as a child; but when I became a man, I put away childish things."

But while the ancients gave little thought to the child *as child,* he figured in their lives in a number of important ways. First of all, he represented fertility, a symbol common to all mankind since prehistoric times. Second, as the laughing child of mythology, Eros or Cupid, he represented sexual love. Third, in those superstitious times he was often thought of as the embodiment of the supernatural. In Rome only youngsters could wear the *toga praetexta,* which was otherwise reserved for priests, and in Egypt they led the sacred bull through town. As Plutarch noted, the Egyptians thought that young people could foretell future events: "They even look upon children as gifted with a kind of faculty of divination, and they are ever anxious to observe the accidental prattle they talk during play, especially if in a sacred place, getting presages of future events."

In more practical terms, adults used children to further their own aims. Through carefully arranged marriages and adoptions they made them the primary channel for acquiring and perpetuating family property. They also used them as political hostages, security for debts, and, in the case of the Babylonians, as negotiable assets which could be sold into slavery for a father's profit. Indeed, throughout the ancient world parents seemed to value children mainly for the services they could provide. Adults relied upon their offspring's unpaid labor for years and then they expected the children to take care of them in old age. When the Greek heroine Medea decides to kill her children in revenge for their father's rejection of her, she only regrets that now no one will be left to take care of *her*. Just before committing the murder, she pauses to lament:

> What was the purpose, children, for which I reared you?
> For all my travail, and wearing myself away?
> They were sterile, those pains I had in the bearing of you.
> Oh surely once the hopes I had, poor me,
> Were high ones; you would look after me in old age,
> And when I died would deck me well with your own hands;
> A thing which all would have done. Oh but it is gone,
> That lovely thought.

CHAPTER THREE

PAGES, MONKS, AND MAIDENS

Ancient times came to an end with the fall of Rome in the fifth century. For the next five hundred years commerce and culture declined in Western Europe. Then in the eleventh century the economy began to expand once again. New wealth was created and with it came renewed interest in the refinements of life. During this vigorous era, which we call the High Middle Ages, progress was made on many fronts, yet the treatment of children remained frozen in the past. Then why dwell on the era? Because in it for the first time we find men choosing to write about domestic life as well as war. When referring to child care, medieval writers were describing its practice among the nobles who were their principal readers. We can assume, however, that many of the attitudes they speak of were also to be found among the peasants.

INFANCY

To protect his clothes from slobber
You will say to his nurse
"Make the child a bib"
—*The Treatise of Walter de Biblesworth,*
early fourteenth century

Medieval man believed in the importance of prenatal influences. Pregnant women were exhorted to think pleasant thoughts, feel exalted emotions and exercise those virtues that would give their unborn children the finest characters. But if a child was conceived at one of the forbidden times in the Christian calendar, no amount of right thinking on his mother's part could rid him of the consequences of his parents' sin. In the opinion of some churchmen, he was marked from the start.

When a woman went into labor, she was entrusted to the care of midwives who had total charge of the delivery. The midwives' knowledge was extremely limited, however, so anything except the most routine delivery was highly precarious. If a baby started to emerge any way but head first, the midwife tried to push the infant back into the womb or change its position with her hands, no instruments having been developed to help her. If all else failed, the child was excised from the body by Caesarean section. Although this operation had been performed since ancient times, the mother always died.

Many babies were scarred for life by the midwives' ineptitude. Others paid a high price for their mother's poor diet, the prevalence of venereal disease, and the fact that so many pregnant women were teenagers who, along with those over thirty-five, still run the greatest risk of having defective offspring. Given these conditions, it is little wonder that medieval children seemed to be afflicted with an appalling incidence of blindness, lameness, maiming, and other physical deformities.

But even when the infant emerged from the womb intact, its life was far from assured. Spoiled food, polluted water, and the bone-chilling dampness of all-stone houses made the young child their particular target. In the cities there was the ever present threat of fire and in the country the ever present threat of famine. During hard times the peasants were reduced to eating roots and bark, and many died. Typhoid, dysentery, bubonic plague, tuberculosis, influenza, and smallpox epidemics devastated whole populations. Poor children must have suffered from these natural disasters and negligent care more than rich children, because, despite the fact that their birth rate was approximately the same, the upper classes left more heirs than the lower classes. Still, only one child out of every two or three could be counted on to live to maturity in the Middle Ages.

Because of this high rate of mortality and possibly for the purpose of preventing infanticide, the Church began to call for the immediate baptism of all infants. Until that time the rite had been performed only at two specified times of the year or in cases of imminent death. In the High Middle Ages baptism was a great event, establishing the legitimacy so crucial to all inheritance and protection in that era. Relatives and vassals were called together as witnesses. One of the youngest—who would presumably outlive the others—might be struck hard with a fist or rewarded with cherries to keep the memory of the event bright in his mind. As time passed, baptisms became so lavish that in some places it was deemed necessary to restrict the outlay by municipal ordinance. One such law in fourteenth-century Nuremberg levied a fine of two florins for decorating christening robes with precious metals or pearls. It also forbade more than twelve guests to attend the baptismal ceremony and then allowed only three of them to be entertained later at the parents' home.

Baptism in the Middle Ages consisted of total immersion to prevent the Evil One from getting even a fingerhold on the soul. Indeed, since the rite was considered a literal exorcism, the child who cried during the ceremony was thought to be letting the devil out. As they held the baby in their arms, the godparents solemnly vowed to protect him from water, fire, horse's foot, and hound's tooth for a period of seven years.

After the ceremony it was common custom to gift the newborn. In the early centuries he was given small symbolic sums of money, salt, bread, and cheese for his journey through life, and throughout the Middle Ages he was often presented with a "teething ring" of stick coral and bells. The coral had been used since ancient times as an amulet against evil spirits as well as for relief in teething, while the bells were supposed to frighten the evil spirits away. Another common gift among the upper classes was a set of twelve "apostle spoons." These spoons were made of silver gilt, each handle fashioned in the shape of a different apostle who was identifiable by his own distinctive emblem. Although this custom began to die out in the mid–seventeenth century, we still use the expression "born with a silver spoon in his mouth" to describe someone who comes from a wealthy family.

Aside from brief periods in his elegant birth robes and christening gown, the medieval child spent the earliest months of his life wrapped up in tight swaddling bands. Swaddling has been one of the most remarkably persistent of man's customs. Ancient Jews, Greeks, and Romans swaddled, as do modern Poles, Japanese, Lapps, and Mexicans. The Infant Jesus was swaddled and so was Russian author Leo Tolstoy. Indeed, so closely is swaddling associated with infancy that when the American Academy of Pediatrics adopted an official insignia, it chose a swaddled babe after the famous Della Robbia medallions that adorn the Ospedale degli Innocenti in Florence.

Over the centuries many reasons have been given for swaddling. The ancients liked it because it seemed to form the body into a straight, pleasing shape. Many mothers liked it because it decreased the baby's demand for her attention. Still others felt it prevented the infant from becoming terrified at the sight of his own limbs. Without swaddling bands, they said, a baby would tear its ears off, scratch its eyes out, touch its genitals, or crawl around on the floor like an animal. Bartholomew, the popular British encyclopedist, set forth the medieval rational for swaddling in 1230:

> And for tenderness the limbs of the child may easily and soon bow and bend and take diverse shapes. And therefore children's members and limbs are bound with lystes [bandages] and other convenable bonds, that they be not crooked nor evil shapen. . . .

The infant was probably totally swaddled for one to four

months, then the arms were freed and the body and legs alone were swaddled for another six to nine months. After they removed the last of the swaddling bands, many peoples continued to restrain the child in a variety of devices. Far from being harmful, swaddling has been shown to have some surprisingly therapeutic effects. A team of American doctors who studied the practice in 1964 showed clinically that swaddled infants sleep more than nonswaddled, their hearts beat more slowly, they cry less and they become generally calmer. Indeed, the doctors were so impressed with their findings that they recommended the reintroduction of swaddling for certain fussy babies.

For the first two or three years, the medieval child's major source of nourishment was human milk. We know that peasant and middle-class women suckled their own, but we are less sure about upper-class women. The bulk of the evidence supports the theory that noble ladies gave over their infants to wet nurses. Yet historian Morris Bishop contends that most gentlewomen did their own nursing lest their offspring become contaminated by less-than-royal milk. He cites the case of Blanche of Castile, who caught a commoner nursing a royal child. Horrified, Blanche turned the infant upside down until he vomited.

Medieval people were rightly suspicious of cow and goat's milk, which carried the tuberculosis bacillus and other germs. Yet they must have resorted to it rather frequently, because their literature lists the nursing horn among the necessary equipment for a baby nurse. Infant feeding vessels had been made in a variety of materials and shapes since their introduction at least two thousand years before Jesus. In the Middle Ages people preferred to use a small polished cow's horn. They pierced a hole in the narrow end of the horn, then fastened two small, finger-shaped pieces of parchment over it. The infant sucked on these "nipples" to get his milk.

Children were nursed for a much longer period in the Middle Ages than they are today, anywhere from one to three years, with boys being weaned a full year later than girls.* Early on, though, their milk was supplemented with solid food. At first this food consisted solely of a watery gruel, but soon it included most items on the regular adult diet. Mothers and wet nurses chewed tough foods before giving them to the toothless baby, a practice still being followed by many isolated peoples.

Many babies slept in rocking cradles which were used from the early Middle Ages. They were made of carved or plain wood and were often topped by a hood to keep out drafts. In those days cradles were more than just a convenience or a status symbol—they were often a matter of life and death. Clergymen urged that children be put in them until the age of three to avoid the "overlaying" or suffocation of infants that often resulted from the common practice of taking very small children into their caretaker's bed. Parents and wet nurses were exhorted not to coddle young children "like the ivy that certainly kills the tree encircled by it, or the ape that hugs her welps to death with mere fondness."†

During the first seven years of life, which medieval man conceptualized in a general way as "infancy," children were left almost exclusively in the care of women. Men were too busy working and warring to bother much about them. Just who these women caretakers were is not clear, but it would seem that many of them were not the children's own biological mothers. In those days so many women died in childbirth that a large number of medieval children must have been orphans or semiorphans. The fairy tales and fables which originated in this era often revolve around the consequences of parental loss as embodied in the person of the wicked stepmother. The origins of this archetype can probably be traced to the latent fear we all

---

*We have no explanation for this disparity, but it could stem from a greater concern with the survival of the male child, who was more important to medieval society than the female.

†A recent medical report casts doubt on the age-old suffocation theory. Its author, Dr. J. Bruce Beckwith, suggests that the unexpected death of healthy infants in their sleep was actually caused by the recently identified and still imperfectly understood phenomenon, Sudden Infant Death Syndrome (SIDS) or "crib death."

have of losing our mothers and also to the real-life loss sustained by so many youngsters throughout the Middle Ages and earlier eras.

Every day during those first seven years and on a more limited basis after that, the more privileged medieval children played games and amused themselves with toys. And a rich variety of toys it was. The children were provided with clay animals of every species, wooden hobbyhorses, and whole armories of weapons, windmills (which had just been invented) and, for both boys and girls, dolls of both refined and rough manufacture. In castle courtyards and on village greens, the little ones amused themselves by marching about in military formations and playing tag, follow-the-leader, hide-and-seek, and leapfrog. At other times they made mud pies or sang, danced and played instruments.

During their early years children were little noticed by society. As late as the sixteenth century the French essayist Montaigne casually remarked of his own baby, "I don't count the little one." The reason for this offhand attitude was that childhood illnesses were often fatal in those prevaccine days and more young children died than lived. Since childhood diseases tend to strike in the first seven years of life, society saw no point in making any emotional or educational investment in a youngster until he had survived them. But after his seventh birthday, when it looked as though he would live to maturity, the child was taken in hand. According to medieval custom, he was now expected to learn and produce at the same time.

SERVICE

During the Middle Ages and for a long time thereafter, the rule for every child—highborn or lowborn, male or female, town sophisticate or country bumpkin—was apprenticeship. Children were expected to learn through practice while at the same time making a contribution to society at large. Apprenticeship was the universal form of education. Even for those to whom formal schooling was important, such as clerics, service was as much a part of the curriculum as rhetoric.

For the upper classes, service was interpreted as domestic work. Nor were these chores considered to be undignified or degrading. Starting in the Dark Ages, boys were sent to the home of a relative or overlord where they were taught "manners," then the whole of social intercourse. They learned how to set a table, carve and serve a joint of meat, make up a bed, groom the horses, and dress the lord in his heavy armor. These page boys—part servant, part privileged student—were also trained in riding, fencing, hunting, hawking, and the arts of war. In this way they became thoroughly imbued with the ideals of their class: loyalty to the Church, obedience to the lord and lady, adherence to the code of chivalry.

Girls were also sent to other castles. They were called bower maidens (bower being the name of a lady's private chamber) or maids of honor, and they, too, were expected to learn by doing. Besides performing personal services for their mistresses, the girls were taught how to curtsy gracefully, how to preserve fruit and make perfumes, and how to sing and dance in a pleasing manner. They also became expert in the spinning, weaving, sewing, and embroidery that were the eternal lot of women in those days. In addition, they were schooled in the art of healing. The medieval girl was taught how to bandage wounds, use splints, prepare medicinal drafts from herbs and how "to succor the men on whose lives her life depended."

Although girls went along on hunting parties and many could ride with the best, by and large they were not given the same vigorous training as boys. In one medieval *geste des dames,* the tale of Galeran, the heroine complains of having nothing to do with her day

> . . . but read my psalter, work in gold and silk, listen to the tales of Thebes and Troy, and play lays on my harp, and checkmate some one else at chess, or feed my little bird upon my fist; I have often heard my master say that such habits come of gentle nurture.

Neither the boys nor the girls acquired much formal education at the castle. The chaplain or a local nun might teach them their ABCs, some Latin, and their psalms, but few children went beyond that. Only a handful were what we would call "educated."

An alternative to castle life for the sons of noblemen was the monastery. While some chose it voluntarily in their teens to escape the upheavals and falsities of everyday life, others, perhaps the majority, had been offered up by their parents in infancy. It must have been a frightening experience for the little oblate, only seven years old or younger, to be delivered to the strange, forbidding-looking monastery where he would spend the rest of his life. No sooner had he arrived than his head was shaved and his clothes exchanged for the monk's cowl. As Orderic described the ordeal in his *Ecclesiastical History:* "So, weeping, my father gave me, a weeping child, into the care of the monk, Reginald, sent me away into exile for love of Thee, and never saw me again."

In the more austere monasteries, the children's lives were rigorous, minutely supervised, and without a single outlet for youthful high spirits. The young oblates rose at two or three in the morning for Matins and Lauds and continued to take part in communal prayer for much of the day. The boys always had a master between them and they could go nowhere, not even to the latrine, without his accompaniment. According to a common rule, no one but the abbot, prior, or master could "make a sign to them or smile to them." Moreover, they were beaten regularly. In the poorer or work-oriented orders, the oblates did manual labor. In the intellectual orders they learned the arts of calligraphy and illumination, for which all civilization can be grateful.

Like their brothers, many upper-class girls who were unmarriageable or otherwise considered "surplus" were offered to the Church. Their orders were generally less austere than those of the men and their lives in many ways more pleasant. Some nuns, such as Chaucer's fashionable prioress, wore elegant habits and valuable jewelry and kept pets. They spent their days teaching school and doing fine needlework. Although the nuns were bound for life, their lot does not compare too unfavorably with that of the average medieval girl who had to marry a man she barely knew and then produce numerous babies, most of whom died in infancy. 2003423

For the peasants childhood was especially brief. Even the littlest ones were sent out to weed, plant, and harvest. Every now and again a peasant child who showed intellectual promise would be trained for a clerical profession by the local priest, but most village children simply followed their parents into the fields. Sometimes a father bound out an extra daughter as a servant in the household of a somewhat wealthier neighbor. According to Bartholomew, this type of bondswoman was made to do the hardest work, "toylynge and slubberynge." She was given exceptionally rough, plain food to eat and "kepte lowe under the yoeke of thraldom and of servage."

Boys of the middle classes had more choice of career than either their noble or peasant counterparts, because in addition to becoming monks or priests, they might become lawyers, merchants, or tradesmen. To follow their chosen careers they, too, were sent away from home. In the Middle Ages a boy spent an average of seven years learning a craft, but some apprenticeships lasted as few as three years and some as many as eleven, depending on the specialty. During this time the apprentice lived with his master's family in quarters which were adjacent to and often hard to distinguish from the place of business. The apprentice had to swear to serve his master "well and truly," keep his secrets, and foreswear brawling, drinking, and low company. The master in return provided bed, board, clothing, and tutelage. Should the master abuse his young helper, the lad could appeal to higher authorities. In London he had recourse to the mayor and aldermen, all of whom had been apprentices themselves and were not always disposed to rule in favor of the master.

Some guilds and companies had very precise and sometimes

eccentric requirements. London clothes workers, for example, would accept as apprentices only those who were "clean of limb and body, and well formed," and the ironmongers had a bylaw forbidding excessively long hair. A number of guilds that specialized in delicate articles requiring dexterity in their manufacture were composed wholly of women. There were fifteen such guilds in Paris at the end of the thirteenth century.

Sometimes indoctrination into a life of service was carried on at home. Mothers prepared their daughters to manage households, merchants used their own sons in the shop counting, weighing, and selling, and some nobles kept their sons at the family fief, bringing in experts to train them there. But the general rule in many European countries was to send children away from home at an early age. An oft-quoted and disparaging description of this practice was written by an Italian visitor to England in the fifteenth century:

> The want of affection in the English is strongly manifested towards their children; for after having kept them at home till they arrive at the age of seven or nine years at the utmost, they put them out, both males and females, to hard service in the houses of other people, binding them generally for another seven or nine years. And these are called apprentices, and during that time they perform all the most menial offices; and few are born who are exempted from this fate, for everyone, however rich he may be, sends away his children into the house of others, whilst he, in return, receives those of strangers into his own. And on inquiring their reason for this severity, they answered that they did it in order that their children might learn better manners. But I, for my part, believe that they do it because they like to enjoy all their comforts themselves, and that they are better served by strangers than they would be by their own children.

Parents might have had other reasons, too, for sending their offspring away. They might have done it to remove the boys from the feminizing influence of female relatives, as Morris Bishop suggests, and they might have wanted to save themselves the trouble of child rearing. Unfortunately, we can only guess at their motives, because medieval people did not consider service worthy of detailed written explanations. But one thing does seem clear: the parent-child relationship of the Middle Ages was not as emotionally charged as it is today. For when "family" came to mean a personal, sentimental grouping—as opposed to the impersonal, feudal idea of the "line"—parents stopped sending their young children away.

NO GENERATION GAP

The medieval child was brought into the adult world with no intermediate period of preparation and no taboos. He was not shielded from the facts of life, nor could he be, given the crowded living conditions that prevailed during this era. There was no such thing as a separate bedroom, for example; even the great nobles had only two or three rooms and each one of them was used for several purposes, including sleeping. During the day a child mixed with the servants and retainers who swarmed about the castle. At night he slept in a bed with his parents or siblings, at the foot of his parents' bed, or on the floor of the great hall with the servants.

In the workshops, on the battlefields, in the granaries, and at the cookfires, children worked shoulder to shoulder with adults. In this way there was a constant, natural give-and-take between the generations. First the apprentice mixed paints for the master artist, then the artist instructed him in their application. Of course, some consideration was given to the child's lack of background—as with any greenhorn—but medieval society was more concerned with personal capabilities than with age in its expectation and evaluation of performance.

In the relatively few schools, too, all ages mixed unselfconsciously. Children barely out of their "infancy" and grandfathers almost into their dotage sat side by side on the floor at the foot of their master. In the twelfth century Robert of

Salisbury observed: "I saw the students in the school. Their numbers were great. I saw there men of diverse ages: *pueros, adolescentes, juvenes, senes.*" There were two prime reasons for this wide age range. One was that medieval society did not regard school as the unequivocal preparation for life that we do today. In that era people often did things before or during their education. The second reason was that there was no idea that certain subjects—the easier ones—should be studied before other subjects. Indeed, there was no set curriculum: the student could start with any subject and follow it up with any other.

As a result of this system, the more competent student was distinguished from the less competent not by the courses he took, for they were the same, but by the number of times he had repeated them. Learning by repeating goes back to ancient times, as we have seen. But it was particularly valuable in the Middle Ages, when books were scarce—the master might own the only copy of a text—and students had to rely on their own memories for information. Learning by repeating also eliminated the need for correspondence between competency and level of teaching. It would take many centuries for educators to evolve the concept of "class," a term denoting a place, an age, and the difficulty of subject matter. The class is the basis for our own homogeneous school groupings, but in those fledgling days of education, it was both unknown and unnecessary.

Students of diverse ages were as close out of school as in it. They lived together, ate together, and took their entertainment together. Medieval scholars deserved their reputation for heavy drinking, and they were often to be found carousing in the local taverns. College drinking songs originated in this era, as students as young as twelve sang, "*Meum est propositum in taberna mori*" ("It's my firm intention in a barroom to die").

In the world outside the college, children and adults also shared lusty pleasures as well as tamer pastimes. To be sure, there were some toys that were reserved for the littlest ones, but adults took part in a lot of what we would now consider "childish" play. They joined in hide-and-seek, blindman's buff, and other ancient games of chasing, hiding, and fighting. A medieval Book of Hours shows an entire village of men, women, and children engaged in a rousing snowball fight. Conversely, children participated actively in what we now consider strictly "adult" games. Gambling, for example, was a grand passion of the times, and medieval children entered enthusiastically into games of cards, dice, backgammon, chess, and cockfights—and they bet heavily on the outcome, too. Society saw nothing corrupt in these pastimes. Moreover, the notion of children as innocents whose virtue had to be protected had not yet gained wide acceptance. Even the Church, which condemned all games out of hand, would have had them banned fully as much for adults as for children.

Another favorite communal pastime of the Middle Ages was listening to a good story. Since the long winter nights were often dull in both castle and village, people eagerly awaited the arrival of an itinerant minstrel or storyteller to entertain them. From all accounts these men were spellbinders. They recounted in lurid detail the heroic deeds of King Arthur and the Knights of the Round Table, the quest of Parsifal, and the passion and betrayal of Tristan and Isolde. Eventually, such epics would be relegated to the status of children's "classics," but in the Middle Ages they constituted *the* people's literature. The hours of pleasure they gave to young and old alike forged yet another bond between the generations.

TOWARD A NEW SENSIBILITY

During much of the thousand years that, for want of a better name, we call the Middle Ages, attitudes toward children were closer to primitive instinct than to modern sensibility. The child was nurtured only on condition—on condition that it was of the proper sex, that economic conditions were good, that it had no mark of the devil on it, and that it was not the product of an illicit union. Early care was based on ancient traditions which were sometimes harmful and often quite useless. Whether from ignorance or willfulness, medieval parents seemed to neglect their babies to an appalling degree.

If superstition and old wives' tales marked the youngsters' early nurture, disfranchisement and brutality often marked their later treatment. Legally, children were put in the same class as servants who had no civil rights. Since they were considered their parents' personal property, youngsters were often disposed to monastery or marriage without even being consulted on the matter. But worst of all, they were freely beaten. This practice was justified on the same religious, moral, and educational grounds that had been cited in ancient times. Philip of Navarre even went so far as to say that "the father who spares the rod does not love his child."

When something was not being done directly to or for the child, he was ignored or, more precisely, not seen. Indeed, he was considered so unimportant that he went almost unrecorded in the art and literature of the period. The child might be perceived as what he would become—warrior, carpenter, parent, servant—but he was never recognized for what he was: a unique personality at a certain moment in his development. Indeed, in that era when every nuance of social standing was reflected in vestiary adornment, there was no such thing as a child's costume. Once out of infancy, the child was dressed exactly like an adult of his social class.

But a change in attitude was in the offing because of certain profound cultural movements. The first of these was chivalry. Chivalry was a code of honor that advocated gentility and the revolutionary concept of good sportsmanship. It demanded service to those above and responsibility to those below. Chivalry's derivative, courtly love, inspired an esteem for women that had never been known before. Indeed, during the High Middle Ages women were elevated to that pedestal from which some of them are now trying to descend. The new, protective attitude toward women was soon extended to children, as evidenced by the chivalric motto, "Women and children first."

Courtly love also influenced the personalization of religion. This was a far cry from the austere worship of earlier centuries. Before, Jesus had been thought of solely as the all-seeing, all-powerful judge of the world, and the art of the times had reflected this. In a typical early icon, for example, Jesus had been shown sitting on his mother's lap, his feet symmetrically balanced, his right hand raised in a symbolic gesture of blessing, his grown-man's face composed into a serious expression. He and the Virgin Mary both stared straight ahead, seemingly oblivious to each other. The lack of communication between them heightened the desired impression of majestic isolation.

Then slowly in the twelfth and thirteenth centuries a new image of Jesus began to emerge: the Divine Child as joyous *bambino*. Instead of a minigod, he was now portrayed as a typical child, one who lies naturally across his mother's lap, swings his feet and glances mischievously from the canvas. Jesus and his mother look at each other with expressions of tenderness on their faces.

People suddenly wanted to find out everything they could about Jesus' life on earth, especially his childhood years. They created a cult of the Infant Jesus, which became the single most important factor in improving the status of children. From a special sympathy for the Holy Child, Western man eventually developed a general sympathy for every child.

THE RENAISSANCE

Starting in Italy in the thirteenth century, Europe began to experience that cultural surge known as the Renaissance. It was a time of scientific discoveries, practical inventions, voyages to unknown lands, and artistic endeavors of almost unparalleled scope and quality. Gorgeous buildings were erected and magnificent frescoes, statues, and paintings were created to decorate them. Men began to think less about their future in heaven and more about their present life on earth.

But for the most part the period's great intellectual and artistic ferment did not engender any new consideration of children. There was little measurable improvement in their status, and the feelings extended to them can best be described as indifferent. As British historian Antonia Fraser put it: "The Renaissance period appears to be singularly lacking in interest in the flowering of the child, apparently absorbed in the flowering of man."

Much of the cultural activity of the Renaissance was paid for by the noveaux riches who benefited from the economic expansion of the times. The new rich made their money in trade and lived in city houses, but they aped the customs of the old medieval nobles who had been supported by farming and had lived in country castles. One of the "noble" customs they liked best was hiring wet nurses, and they didn't care a fig for the women's supposedly polluted milk.

In Italy some wet nurses lived right in the homes of their patrons, but this was not generally considered an ideal arrangement. It crowded the already tight living space and presented another mouth to feed. Far superior, to the Renaissance way of thinking, and far more common, was the practice of sending out an infant to a peasant woman called a *bália*, who lived some distance away in the country. The infant's stay with the *bália* usually lasted two years, but it could vary from a few months to six, ten, or even twelve years if the child could not be accommodated at home. Since a *bália*'s pregnancy led to the termination of the relationship, babies often had to adjust to more than one wet nurse before being weaned and returned to their parents. But from the great popularity of the system, this does not seem to have been viewed as an overriding drawback.

Moralists who urged maternal feeding to no avail also tried unsuccessfully to get parents to visit their babies, but there is little evidence of such visits. Indeed, parents seem to have been indifferent to their offspring's fate. And what must that fate have been without parental supervision? At best the over-worked *bália* might have attempted to do a conscientious minimum in between her household and farm chores. At worst she might have allowed the child to die from neglect. Although wet nurses have been accused of deliberately smothering chil-dren or carelessly running the risk of it, this seems unlikely, since the arrangement was profitable both to her and to her husband. Moreover, the penalties for infanticide could be harsh. One woman who drowned a child was first led through the streets with the dead body tied to her neck and was then burned at the stake for the crime.

At some point those children who survived the stay with the *bália* were returned to their parents. It must have been a great wrench for them to leave the only mother, father, and home they had ever known. The adjustment to their new surround-ings must have been difficult, too, because urban Italian "fami-lies" of the Renaissance often included cousins, aunts, uncles, half sisters, and half brothers. These complicated households were made even more confusing by the presence of free and slave servants of all ages. Nor was this the last adjustment the children would have to make. Renaissance families often had to pull up stakes at short notice and move on to new homes in order to escape plague and political upheavals.

Yet despite these traumatic events, the children survived and often flourished. Surely this raises important historical and psychological questions. As Professor James Bruce Ross asked: "How could the deprived and neglected infants of the middle classes develop into the architects of a vigorous, pro-ductive and creative era which we call 'the Renaissance'?"

Not only is it remarkable that a number of these people became artists, given their early childhood experiences, but that they became artists who were fascinated by—if not obsessed with—the complementary themes of mother love and happy childhood. Over a period of three hundred years they turned out thousands of pictures of the Virgin Mary, the Infant Jesus, holy children, and angel children, as well as countless portraits of ordinary mothers, young children, and adolescents.

While working up their studies, Renaissance artists made some of the first scientific observations of children. Dr. Thomas A. Cone, Jr., claims that the fifteenth-century painter Fra Filippo Lippi was the first to portray the Infant Jesus in accurate proportions, that is, with the head equaling one-quarter the body length instead of the customary one-sixth.

But while these renderings may have been anatomically true to nature, they were not true to life. Renaissance paintings showed babies in the nude and very active, yet in real life those same babies would have been covered up and immobilized by swaddling bands. Artists' babies were always chubby and happy; in real life they were often underfed, unchanged, and quite miserable. And while in reproductions a baby always held its mother's undivided attention, in real life the child would have been miles away from her sight and probably her thoughts as well.

How is it that artists who had never known maternal intimacy themselves nor could even observe it with their own offspring would so persistently portray it? We can only speculate. Perhaps they were acting out a wish fulfillment, a fantasy, to compensate for the deprivation they had experienced as children. Or they might have been consciously fulfilling the emotional needs of mothers whose babies were far from home. It seems likely, too, that they had adopted the new softer attitude toward children, an attitude their art would in turn help to popularize.

With the new artistic sentimentality toward children, civilization was approaching a turning point in the history of feeling. Childhood as a historical concept had not yet arrived, but by 1600 it was well on its way.

A little Egyptian girl's treasures, including a ring, string of shells, and an earring. They were buried with her in this toy basket. (The Metropolitan Museum of Art.)

Detail of a Greek vase showing young athletes practicing. (The Metropolitan Museum of Art.)

Detail of an early fourteenth-century painting in which the Virgin Mary and Jesus seem unaware of one another. Although obviously a baby, Jesus has the face of a mature man. (The Metropolitan Museum of Art.)

Two hundred years later we see how art, sentiment, and religion had progressed to the point where Mary and her son are portrayed in loving relationship to one another. (The Metropolitan Museum of Art.)

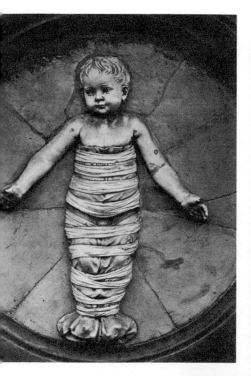

Swaddling bands were removed in successive stages, as we can see from these famous reliefs sculpted for a foundling hospital in Italy. (The Bettmann Archive Inc.)

This German woodcut catches the essence of education in 1500—and 1900—learning enforced by the master's rod or switch. Note the low benches. Until modern times many scholars literally sat at their masters' feet. (The Pierpont Morgan Library.)

In the illustration below from a Dutch book of 1618, we get some idea of the rich variety of games children played. Note, too, how elaborately the youngsters were dressed. (The Pierpont Morgan Library.)

CHAPTER FOUR

FROM RENAISSANCE TO ROUSSEAU

At the opposite end of the spectrum from artistic sentimentality was the new belief in the power of human reason that grew up as the Renaissance waned. The Enlightenment, as this rational approach to the universe was called, led to great changes in the religion, politics, science, and education of the seventeenth and eighteenth centuries. It also contributed to a new awareness of the child. As we can see from the art of the period, the child was starting to be thought of as a distinctive and not unimportant individual.

FIRST SIGNS

During the Renaissance it had been common for middle-class adults to commission portraits of themselves, but no one thought to commission portraits of their children. The fleeting state of childhood was considered too unimportant to record, whether the individual lived beyond it or died while in it. The Infant Jesus had been a favorite subject of artists, of course, and anonymous children had appeared in crowd scenes. But it took some time until real children, too, began to be reproduced.

They made their first appearance in Western art on the tomb sculptures of their teachers and parents. Both surviving and deceased children were included, the dead youngsters being the smaller figures with a cross or skull in their hands. When middle-class men donated stained-glass windows or paintings to local churches, they often had themselves painted into the religious scene. After a time, their families were painted in with them.

When artists moved the location of their paintings indoors, family scenes became a favorite subject. At first these were stiff, posed-looking works, but in time they became almost snapshots of domestic activity. They were the forerunners of the family photo album that can be found in almost every home today. And the desire to have such a personal visual record seems to have stemmed from the same emotional wellspring: a sentimental feeling about home and the family. The child was part and parcel—if not yet the focal point—of that feeling. Portraits of children apart from their parents were a rarity until the end of the sixteenth century, but after that they were very common. Suddenly it seemed very important to capture for all time the picture of a child *as* a child, before he grew out of that state or died.

Another sign of an awakening perception of childhood was the assignment of a special costume to young people. In medieval times all ages within the same social class had worn the same outfits. But from the late 1500s on, wealthy and middle-class parents no longer dressed their children in miniature replicas of their own clothes. Rather, they put them in special dress reserved for their age group alone. Since a great deal of importance was attached to clothing as a barometer of social standing, this children's costume proclaimed to all that childhood—at least among the upper classes—was now a separate entity.

There were other indications, too, of a widening generation gap. Whereas all ages had entered freely into communal recreation during the Middle Ages, betting and other pastimes came to be considered inappropriate for children, while hoop rolling and other games were increasingly thought too childish for adults. Stories which were once intended to appeal both to adults and children were now reserved solely for one group or the other. Thus, fairy tales came to belong just to children while the classics in their original form became the exclusive property of adults. Children were allowed to hear these stories only in expurgated form.

Not every one of the foregoing changes could be considered a plus for children, but developments in yet another area, that of medicine, could only accrue to their benefit. In the seventeenth century pediatrics had but one direction to go and that direction was up.

CHILD CARE: SPIDERS AND PSEUDOSCIENCE

I know very well in how unbeaten and almost unknown a Path I am treading; for sick Children, and especially Infants, give no other Light into the Knowledge of their Diseases, than what we are able to discover from their uneasy Cries, and the uncertain Tokens of their Crossness; for which Reason, several Physicians of the first Rank have openly declared to me, that they go very unwillingly to take care of the Diseases of Children, especially such as are newly born, as if they were to unravel some strange Mystery, or cure some incurable Disease.

—Walter Harris, British pediatrician, 1689

In some places in some eras doctors were paid less for treating a slave than a free man and nothing at all for a sick child. The low status assigned to medical care for children continued right into modern times. To be sure, even the ancient Egyptians had identified certain diseases of childhood and had discussed the best methods of infant care. But for some fourteen hundred years after the fall of Rome, so-called men of science did little more than copy and translate the medical advice of the ancients.

Then, in the seventeenth century, some men began to observe human bodies in a scientific manner. They managed to unravel a number of physiological mysteries, but their efforts were hampered by the taboos and superstitions which governed people's thinking. Men were not allowed at the delivery of a baby, for example, because their presence was considered bad luck and women became unusually modest during labor. So strong was this prohibition that when a Dr. Wertt of Hamburg was found trying to observe a delivery disguised as a woman, he was convicted and burned to death!

Lacking the facts which only firsthand, trained observation could bring, people fell back on folklore. Their superstitious ideas seem unbelievably primitive to us, but long usage gave them the ring of truth to their practitioners. The child's sex was supposedly determined by what the pregnant woman ate, for example, a lean diet producing boys, a rich one girls. This belief is the basis for our nursery rhyme: "What are little boys made of? Snips and snails and puppy dog tails" and "What are little girls made of? Sugar and spice and everything nice." Birth injuries and malformations were often attributed to the pregnant woman's vivid imagination. In one instance it was reported that a newborn resembled a lion-monster. Cause: the mother's visit to the Tower while pregnant, "where she was much terrify'd with the old lion's noise."

Infant care continued in age-old patterns, too. For example, the infant was swaddled and seems to have been infrequently washed. Indeed, as late as the eighteenth century washing a child's head was considered the surest way to give him a cold. Instead, mothers protected their babies' heads with a cap which was worn indoors and out. Perhaps as a result of this practice, infants' scalps were frequently described by contemporaries as being covered with scales and other itchy eruptions. Another ancient feature of infant care, drugging a fitful child with liquor, was also continued in the post-Renaissance era. As one writer advised:

> Good Cordials give it, such as bear the Name
> Of him whose Glory rival'd *Pompey's* Fame . . .
> Nor is it ill to cheer its Heart with Wine;
> For of all Cordials, that's the most divine.

When a child became ill, the best doctor for him or her was said to be an old woman. People reasoned that even if the woman did little good, at least she would do no great harm, while doctors, who regularly bled their patients, very well might. The recommended remedies for whooping cough indicate the level of her healing arts. They included carrying the afflicted child through a cloud of smoke, placing a live frog in his mouth, or holding an old spider over his head while saying the charmed words:

> Spider, as you waste away,
> Whooping cough no longer stay.

CHILD DEVELOPMENT AND DISEASES

Because they had not systematically observed many children, doctors had little notion of what was normal behavior and what was not. The diary of Héroard, private physician to the future King Louis XIII, contains many of the mistaken ideas of the time. Héroard made nine thousand entries in his diary, covering every aspect of Louis's first twenty-six years of life. In the beginning of this remarkable account, Héroard notes Louis's strong desire to suck. But by mistaking this perfectly natural drive for persistent hunger, the doctor had the little prince consistently overstuffed with milk.

Hiccups, another harmless natural phenomenon, were of concern to doctors who said they might prove deadly if they continued and were attended by complications. Robert Pemell, a British pediatrician, recommended that the child afflicted with "the Hicket" be induced to vomit "by putting down a feather annointed with oyl. . . ." Pemell attributed many dire consequences to teething, also, and he was not alone in this belief. The British Bills of Mortality from 1701 to 1776 ascribed 90,000 deaths to teething—a perfectly normal part of growing up.

The Bills of Mortality more accurately attest to the dismaying frequency with which great epidemics swept across Europe in the seventeenth century, attacking adults and children alike. The plague, leprosy, typhus, typhoid fever, smallpox, and influenza caused the deaths of thousands at a time. Gastrointestinal upsets, too, seemed to have been frequent and fatal, and diarrhea made infants its particular victims in the hot summer months. The Bills of Mortality listed these infant killers under such colorful names as Flux, Watery Gripes, Twisting of the Gut, and Stoppage in the Stomach. Measles and whooping cough also attacked children in large numbers and were far more serious—if not fatal—then than now.

All of the foregoing diseases were the work of nature, but some others were caused or assisted by man. Rickets, for example, became widespread among children in the English countryside when their parents set them to work spinning and weaving wool inside their cottages. Kept indoors all day, the children were deprived of the vitamin D provided by sunshine, and without it, their bones softened and became deformed. Later, when children were employed in urban factories, rickets became a disease of the towns.

But even before that time, the cities were a fertile breeding ground for any number of diseases. The cities were growing by leaps and bounds and the overcrowding in the poorer sections was fierce. Moreover, since the new city dwellers did not know how or have the facilities to eliminate waste, the filth both inside the homes and on the streets was atrocious. Contagious diseases had a field day in these dirty and crowded slums. And many children died from tetanus or lockjaw after dirt had gotten into a cut. The cities did not have a monopoly on malnutrition, of course, but their inhabitants were more likely to suffer periods of deprivation than country folk who could raise their own food. City children—and their parents—regularly starved to death.

Although children still were not considered important enough to occupy a prominent place in their parents' letters, when they were mentioned it was often in the setting of a sickroom. The parents reacted to their children's illnesses in a variety of ways from tremendous worry to callous disinterest. Some simply declared it a matter for God and therefore out of human hands. But alongside these age-old attitudes a new feeling began to appear, the feeling that diseases should be controlled, that the tragic toll of young lives should be reduced. There was a growing confidence that men *could* make a difference.

ADVICE AND PROGRESS

The first book of pediatrics in the English language was written by Dr. Thomas Phayre in 1545, *The Regiment of Life, whereunto is added a treatise of pestilence, with the boke of children.* Dr. Phayre announced his purpose in writing it as "here to do them good that have most need, that is to say children." The *Boke of Children* remained popular for over a hundred years. But typical of that era, it was essentially a copy of earlier translations, which, in turn, were based on the ancients.

At about the same time as Phayre, a Frenchman was dispensing similar advice in Latin verse. Pediatric poems had been known from the Middle Ages, but Scévole de Sainte-Marthe's rhymes were so popular that he has been called the "Dr. Spock of the sixteenth century." More and more children were being fed by sucking cans, spoons, and filled linen bags. But Sainte-Marthe, like every other writer up to that point, advocated maternal breast feeding to be given on demand:

> Twas a *Sage* said it, and the Saying's good,
> The Mother's Milk's the only wholesome Food.
> Large Meals upon the Sucking Babe bestow,
> And freely let the Snowy Fountains flow. . . .
>
> The Hours for Suckling I do not fix,
> Nature in that must guide the nursing Six.

When by its Cries it calls you, do not spare
Your Labour, nor be loath your Breast to bare.

While Sainte-Marthe was dispensing his homely poetic advice, doctors of a more scientific bent were beginning to study their small patients closely. Their clinical observations enabled them to accurately describe—and therefore start to cure—such childhood afflictions as rickets. During this period, too, forceps were invented, which aided in the delivery of babies. And by the end of the seventeenth century, child-care manuals were making their way into more homes than ever before, thanks to the development of the printing press. These manuals, advances in pediatric medicine, and a growing interest in childhood were all leading up to better general care for children. Good care, though, was still a long way off.

EDUCATION

In addition to medical inquiry, the Enlightenment fostered a tremendous surge of interest in education. English Puritans and reform French Catholics both saw education as a way to remove the child from this depraved world and prepare him for the next purer one. Philosophers promoted it as the road to universal moral improvement, and middle-class parents seized upon it as a means of advancing their sons in the world. Girls benefited much less from the academic excitement, because their lives still revolved around the home.

Education was becoming the way to secure important government posts and other economically advantageous positions. It was also the avenue to upward social mobility. Since education was thought necessary by the English to develop a child into a gentleman, or gentlewoman, the new bourgeoisie tried to imitate the bookishness of the landed gentry. They were aided in this ambition by the tremendous expansion of the English school system that saw a grammar school established within twelve miles of almost every family. In France the Jesuits took the lead in providing primary schools for village children of modest circumstances and secondary education for the wealthier boys.

With the spread of education came the idea that education should be for the young, and the young alone. Adult education, which had been widespread in the fifteenth and sixteenth centuries, disappeared in the seventeenth. In the Middle Ages, school was not the only preparation for "life," because some people worked first, then studied, or regularly alternated the two. Now, as the school cycle lengthened, the idea of apprenticing first was eliminated. Between the seventeenth century and the early years of the nineteenth, the following comment by a school inspector remained valid: "Children cannot be sent to school before the age of seven or eight. . . . At the age of eleven or twelve, they are sent to work."

After the idea took hold that education was for the young exclusively, age groupings became more and more homogeneous within the school setting. Gone was the free and easy mixing of ages when old men and young boys sat side by side at the foot of an independent master. Nevermore would they share lodgings in a boarding house or stand one another to drinks in the local tavern as they had in the Middle Ages. The change was gradual. At first the students were grouped according to "age and development," but "development" or capabilities still counted most. Then, between the seventeenth and nineteenth centuries, age became the most important factor. The most precocious and most tardy were dropped and "class" came to mean an age group as well. Gradually, too, everyone of the same age was considered to have the same capacity for learning, so that a student was rarely allowed to advance faster than his peers, no matter how bright he was.

One of the reasons people of different ages had been able to mix so freely in medieval colleges was that there had been no set curriculum in which subjects became increasingly more difficult as one ascended. Moreover, students had learned by repetition, so the newcomers were not thought to hold back the more experienced scholars. But by 1550, after some 150 years of evolution, the idea of a regular cycle became established throughout the Western world. All children entered at the sixth or fifth class and progressed upward to the first class or form. A grade was rarely skipped. A master was assigned to each grade and the first attempts were made to tailor his teaching to the students' level. In time the children began to progress in an orderly fashion from primary to secondary to university level and the cycle grew ever longer.

THE THREE R'S—IN LATIN

In Europe children got their first taste of education at home or at small neighborhood schools. In either setting they started out by learning their ABCs, usually through rhymes. Rhyming devices had been used to teach the alphabet for some time, but the first printed example of this technique that we know of dates from 1710. It starts out:

> A was an Archer, and shot at a Frog;
> B was a Blind-man, and led by a Dog:
> C was a Cutpurse, and liv'd in disgrace;
> D was a Drunkard, and had a red Face:
> E was an Eater, a Glutton was he;
> F was a fighter, and fought with a Flea:
> G was a Gyant, and pul'd down a House;
> H was a Hunter, and hunted a Mouse. . . .

When children started school their first "text" was a hornbook. This primer consisted of a wood, leather, or bone tablet into whose recess had been fitted a piece of paper or parchment. The Lord's Prayer, the alphabet, and perhaps a set of Roman numerals were printed or written on the paper. A slice of thin, transparent horn covered the paper to protect it from the student's grimy fingers, much as we might use a plastic protector today. Since none of the surviving hornbooks is identical to any other, one expert speculates that each child may have had one carved especially for his use when he started school. During recess the hornbook had another function: with its short handle it made an ideal bat. When not in use either for reading or for games, the primer hung by a thong from the student's belt.

Originally, the primary schools taught all their subjects in Latin, because the curriculum had been designed with choirboys in mind and Latin was the language of the Church. Thus, children became well versed in religious prayers, chants, and songs from an early age. Indeed, singing remained as important a part of the curriculum as Latin for a long time. In England the little neighborhood schools, which were heir to this religious heritage, were called "song schools," and as late as 1700 in France children were still being taught to read Latin before French. After that time, though, the Latin language was gradually separated from book learning.

As the primary school developed, it continued to teach singing and the rudiments of reading and writing, but other subjects were introduced as well. Etiquette, for example, occupied an important place in these early primary schools. Books of etiquette were used to teach reading, recognition of different styles of writing, and good manners. Reading and writing were not considered two sides of the same coin, as we now think of them, but rather were taught separately. Reading was associated with great literature and religious culture, while writing was associated with manual arts and commerce. Indeed, writing schools taught by master scribes prepared children for trade. Arithmetic, too, was considered background for handling practical, everyday affairs rather than an avenue to theoretical contemplation. As one moved up in grade level, the natural sciences and humanities were introduced to give the children a sense of a unified world order.

One of the most highly stressed areas in education was the moral improvement of students. Educators felt it was their duty to set children on the path to righteousness. They did not take this responsibility lightly for children were then thought to be full of all sorts of evil tendencies which only constant vigilance could combat. One of the most gruesome writers of this era was James Janeway. He did not feel children should play any games, own any toys, or have any fun. For decades young Englishmen had to learn his verses by heart and recite them in front of the class. The following example is typical of his approach:

> The Lord delights in them that speak
>   The Words of Truth; but ev'ry Lyar
> Must have his Potion in the Lake,
>   That burns with Brimstone, and with Fire.
>
> Then let me always watch my Lips,
>   Lest I be struck to Death and Hell
> Since God a Book of Reck'ning keeps
>   For ev'ry Lie that Children tell.

The students reciting those lines were boys, for girls were almost completely left out of the expansion of education. Whether of high or low birth, the girls' training consisted primarily of the domestic arts and only very secondarily of scholastic accomplishment. In fact, they were virtually illiterate. Even those girls who were mandated to convents were taught religious exercises but little else. From the age of ten, girls were considered little women, and it was still the custom to marry them off very early. Therefore, all during this era a girl's childhood was considerably shorter and less scholastic than that of her school-going brother. As the Frenchman Fénelon described this disparity of educational opportunity in the seventeenth century:

> The greatest experts have taken pains to lay down rules in this respect. How many masters and colleges there are! How much

money is spent on the printing of books, on scientific research, on methods of teaching foreign languages, on choosing professors . . . and this shows the high opinion people have of the education of boys. . . . [But] it is considered perfectly permissible to abandon girls willy-nilly to the guidance of ignorant or indiscreet mothers. . . . Teach a girl to read and write correctly. It is shameful but common to see women of wit and manners unable to pronounce what they read: either they hesitate or they read in a sing-song voice. . . . They are even more at fault in their spelling, and in shaping and joining letters of the alphabet when writing.

SCHOOLBOY REBELLIONS

While the master shouts himself hoarse, these lazy children sit dozing and thinking of their pleasures. One boy who is absent has paid one of his companions to answer in his place. Another has lost his breeches, while yet another is looking at his foot which is poking through a hole in his shoe.
—Description of an early sixteenth-century Paris classroom

To the new breed of moralists, the atmosphere described above was intolerable. It smacked of the anarchy of the Middle Ages, an anarchy that offended the reformers' sense of orderliness, discipline, and morality. Over the next 150 years, the moralists relentlessly chiseled away at the roughness of school life. And when they got through, something new had been created: the well-bred schoolboy.

The major strategy the reformers employed was negative reinforcement. Pupils who neglected their appearance were punished. Pupils who changed masters without permission— once an acceptable practice—were punished. Pupils who took absences without permission were punished. But the students seemed quite capable of punishing right back, and the school records of the time are full of stories of revenge-seekers who beat up their masters so severely that the teachers had to send for the police. Moreover the children had more to work with than their bare fists: they were armed.

Jesuit college students, who then ranged in age from about nine to sixteen, were officially prohibited from keeping weapons in their rooms. They were supposed to turn in their swords and firearms upon entering the college and claim them when they left again. Since even five-year-old boys wore swords and knew how to use them in those days, college town authorities seemed most worried about that particular weapon. But after an Oration Father was badly mauled by his pupils in 1661, the High Court of Dijon, France, prohibited "all students to carry sticks, stakes and other offensive weapons in the classrooms of the house of the aforementioned Priests of the Oratory."

Sometimes the students staged strikes and formed picket lines. Often they fomented armed rebellions. Indeed, so common were these violent uprisings that when King George III— who had had to cope with a significant uprising himself—met some boys from Eton, he jokingly asked, "Have you had any mutinies lately, eh, eh?" In a typical rebellion at Die, France, a class barricaded itself inside the college, preventing any other students or masters from entering. The rebels fired pistol shots, threw benches out of windows, tore up books, and upon leaving even attacked some passersby.

By the end of the seventeenth century, French schoolboys no longer engaged in these armed rebellions. From then on when they staged a mass protest, it was likely to be over a political issue, much like a modern peace rally or prowar demonstration. But in England mutinies increased and grew more and more violent. In 1768 the monitors or good pupils of the sixth form—eleven year olds—seceded and left the school. At Winchester the student uprising was so violent that two companies of troops with fixed bayonets had to be called in to suppress it. And at Rugby the pupils first set fire to their books and desks and then withdrew to an island which was wrested from them only by an assault of the army.

Not all of the schoolboys' aggression was directed toward their masters and administrators. Much of it was vented on each other. The Western world was a violent place in those days, a place in which entire trade guilds or whole villages squared off against one another, and, after school, children did the same. At Aix in France there was a great fight between the Philosophy class and the Humanities class, a fight so violent that some of the students were imprisoned. And at Avignon in the same country children attending the Jesuit college battled those studying with master scribes and other pedagogues. A contemporary described these donnybrooks as "fights which distract them from their studies and in which they risk being wounded unto death." Duels were common, too. In a memoir of this era one man mentioned a brother who died "from a sword-thrust when he tried to separate two students who were fighting."

DISCIPLINE

In this rough and tumble era physical force was the major way to enforce social control. When adults misbehaved, they were publicly and cruelly humiliated, and children were certainly given no more consideration. The schoolboys who rebelled and got caught were flogged and the birch still reigned supreme in the classroom. But discipline began well before the first day of school. It began at home, it began early, and it was extremely harsh by modern standards.

As they had since time immemorial, parents considered beating "natural." They truly believed it proceeded from affection and instilled a sense of respect for them in the child's heart. Moreover, they felt this was the best way to discharge their responsibility to God in bringing up a child. According to the religious ideas of the day, parents were just surrogates in this world for His authority in the next. If we take her words at face value, Lady Jane Grey was gratified by her parents' conscientious attention to this duty. Their methods were apparently typical of the sixteenth century:

> One of the greatest benefits that God ever gave me is that he sent me so sharp and severe parents. . . . For when I am in presence either of father or mother, whether I speak, keep silence, sit, stand, or go, eat, drink, be merry or sad, be sewing, playing, dancing, or doing anything else, I must do it, as it were, in such weight, measure, and number, even so perfectly as God made the world, else I am so sharply taunted, so cruelly threatened, yea presently sometimes with pinches, nippes, and bobs, and some ways which I will not name for the honour I bear them, so without measure misordered, that I think myself in hell.

In deference to his exalted station, little Louis XIII was not physically struck as was Lady Jane Grey. Nevertheless, he was not allowed any sign of willfulness, either, and even he could not say "Je veux"—"I want." Just as parents in the ancient world had summoned up visions of terrifying monsters to keep their children in line, Héroard played on Louis's fears to control him. When the child refused to do as the physician wished, Héroard called in one of the tool-carrying laborers who worked about the château. The very sight of the one-eyed mason or the grotesque hunchback was enough to frighten the child into submission. Héroard also stirred up his fears of rain and thunder, the sound of gunfire, and the loss of his penis. Little wonder that by the age of four the prince was perpetually terrified. In his nightly prayers he asked to be protected from all his enemies visible and invisible and the hulking workmen who were called in to threaten him.

Even then, in the beginning of the seventeenth century, Louis's upbringing was considered old-fashioned. To be sure, most people still used leather straps, the birch stick, or the flat palm when they wanted to get a point of order across to their children. But a new tactic was also coming into favor: guilt. Now, not external controls but developing the child's own conscience was considered the best way to promote good behavior. Children were expected to look within themselves. As the mistress of Port-Royal, an innovative French convent school for girls, wrote, "One must strongly encourage the children to know themselves . . . and to plumb to the bottom of their faults."

There had always been a voice or two raised on behalf of more humane treatment of children. Now those isolated voices began to sound like a humming chorus. Although for very different reasons, Catholic reform leaders, Protestant leaders, and rationalist philosophers all began to call for abatement of corporal punishment. In this period an Englishman wrote:

> Throw away Thy Rod,
> Throw away Thy wrath;
>   O My God,
> Take the gentle path.

John Locke, the most influential writer on education in his time, proposed that adults avoid both the rod *and* all rewards. He recommended that adults balance praise for their children's accomplishments with a "cold and neglectful countenance" for their failures. But perhaps the most modern note of all was sounded by a German princess who was willing to give up a portion of that most sacred adult prerogative: control. "I prefer children a little willful," she wrote. "It shows they are intelligent."

ROUSSEAU

Love childhood, indulge its games, its pleasures, and its lovable nature. Who has not looked back with regret on an age when laughter is always on the lips and when the spirit is always at peace? Why take from these little innocents the pleasure of a time so short which ever escapes them . . . ?

—Jean-Jacques Rousseau, *Émile*

In the seventeenth and eighteenth centuries reason was admired above all else. Men thought that right thinking could lift Western civilization out of the darkness of superstition and religious dogma in which it had so long wallowed. As we have just seen, self-control was the primary method of discipline in this Age of Reason. John Locke extended it to other child-rearing practices as well. He advised parents to start instilling self-control in infants by regulating their feeding schedule and not indulging their crying. The first commentator to mention toilet training, he advised sending the child "to stool regularly" to acquire control of his body.

John Locke's *Thoughts Concerning Education* founded an entire tradition of educational theory. It was a tradition concerned mainly with the best and fastest ways to produce rational adult men out of immature children. Moral perfection in a well regulated manhood was the goal. Education was the tool. Indeed, whether followers of this school thought that a child knew no evil, had evil tendencies, or had come into the world in a "fallen state"—as longstanding Christian tradition would have it—they all looked upon education as the instrument of salvation. It was thought to be a sure-fire protection against the world's corrupting influences.

But some people came to feel that education itself was a corrupting influence. They rebelled against the exaltation of reason and promoted the validity of *feelings* instead. They wanted emotions to have full play, to be free of the tyranny of the mind. The Romantics, as they are called, seized upon the child as a symbol of all they believed in: nature, goodness, joy in living, human progress, instinct, and original innocence not original sin. Through their prose and poetry, the Romantics created the Cult of Childhood. It has colored all our thinking about children from that day to this.

One of the earliest Romantics was Jean-Jacques Rousseau. Initially, he had written off education as a manipulative device of an evil society. But after he was asked to write a tract on education, he suddenly changed his tune. He began to say that the right kind of education could be used to better society. Rousseau had no special credentials to dispense educational advice. Indeed, he consigned all five of his illegitimate children to a foundling hospital and had failed miserably as a tutor. Nevertheless, he did not doubt his ability to do the job. And in 1762 he produced *Émile*—one of the most influential books on education ever written.

Émile is based on the unlikely premise that a young man, a tutor, devotes some twenty years of his life to one pupil. The tutor takes the child into the country to get away from the corrupting influences of his family and society. There, Émile learns from nature and only from nature for the first twelve years of his life. After the education of his body comes the education of his mind, but this education bears very little resemblance to any traditional course of studies. Émile is permitted to read *Robinson Crusoe* to familiarize him with survival in the wilderness, but he is given little else. As Rousseau had often stated: "I detest books. . . . Reading is the scourge of childhood. [Books] merely teach us to talk about things we know nothing about." Presumably, direct observation and discussions with his tutor gave Émile all he needed to know about life.

Émile outraged the philosophers because it emphasized feeling over reason, and it outraged the Church because it gave only the scantiest nod to religion. But few people realized then its truly revolutionary thesis: the child was important as himself. He was no longer to be seen in the traditional ways either as a miniature adult or as a blank screen which reflects whatever adults project onto it. From then on he would be considered a self-active soul. Rousseau also emphasized that this soul had a tendency to virtue which had to be carefully nurtured through education. Indeed, he saw the primary purpose of education as identifying and drawing out the special nature of childhood:

> Nature wants children to be children before they are men. If we deliberately pervert this order, we shall get premature fruits which are neither ripe nor well-flavored, and which soon decay. . . . Childhood has ways of seeing, thinking, and feeling peculiar to itself; nothing can be more foolish than to substitute our ways for them.

Rousseau was the first writer of stature to call attention to these special needs of childhood. He put the emphasis on learning about children rather than on controlling them through physical abuse and more "civilized" psychological tortures— an age-old obsession of man. Rousseau encouraged an entirely new interest in the *process* of growing up rather than just in its end product. In this vein he referred sarcastically to the "wisest writers" who "devote themselves to what a man ought to know, without asking what a child is capable of learning. They are always looking for the man in the child, without considering what he is before he becomes a man."

With interest in progress, education, and children at an all-time high, the world was ripe for *Émile*. Consequently, the response to it was immediate and widespread. In England the book influenced some two hundred other tracts before the century was out. People embraced naturalism in child care as if it were a new religion. Many mothers threw away swaddling bands and took to suckling infants who only a year or so earlier they would have sent straight to a wet nurse. Schoolmasters relaxed their discipline and made some attempt to enliven the curriculum. For the first time a large group of people felt that childhood was worthy of the attention of intelligent adults. Nor did the effects of Rousseau's revolution dissipate after a few years. They are still with us, especially in the arguments for and against permissiveness.

With justification Lord Morely called *Émile* "one of the seminal books in the history of literature." He said "it filled parents with a sense of the dignity . . . of their task. . . . It admitted floods of light and air into the tightly closed nurseries and schoolrooms. . . . It was the charter of youthful deliverance."

CHAPTER FIVE

THE CHILD RECOGNIZED

Christopher Columbus only discovered America: I have discovered the Child.
—Victor Hugo

Rousseau might have been the drum major of the new parade, but many marchers were already falling into line when he blew his whistle. Childhood was an idea whose time had come. Although children continued to suffer from adult ignorance and brutality, there was a growing sympathy for them. That sympathy eventually led to a permanent improvement in their condition and to an awareness of their special intellectual capabilities and emotional needs. With this insight came the creation of a separate literature for children.

CHILDREN'S BOOKS

Throughout the centuries books had been too expensive and children too unimportant to warrant the writing of much juvenile literature. Moreover, the little produced expressly for them was always instructional in nature. The best youngsters could hope for was a text in their own language rather than in Latin and one with a picture or two. Occasionally a popular novel such as *Gulliver's Travels* or *Robinson Crusoe* was reissued for children in abridged, illustrated form, but on the whole almost every book put out for youngsters (or adults, for that matter) was expected to impart facts and instill morals.

Then along came John Newbery. Newbery was not the first publisher to appreciate the longing of young people for entertainment in book form, but he was the first to appreciate the profits to be made by producing what children wanted to read, as opposed to what adults considered suitable for them to read. In the preface to one of his earliest works for children, published in 1740, Newbery wrote: "'tis hoped the whole will seem rather an Amusement than a Task." With these words Newbery ushered in a bright, new era in children's literature.

Where John Newbery led, other publishers followed, and he soon had imitators all over Europe. These men put into book form the Mother Goose stories, ABC rhymes, and fairy tales which had been told to children from generation to generation. Along with the old favorites, publishers put out new stories for children, too. Many of them are no longer read, but "The Princess and the Pea," "Thumbelina," and "The Ugly Duckling" by the great Danish storyteller Hans Christian Andersen are as popular with children today as they were when first written. Some new stories featured a device never before seen in literature: the animal narrator. Pigs, cows, goats—even pincushions and bedframes!—began to have their say in books. Although totally fantastical, or perhaps because of it, these stories held young people in their thrall.

In the early days of juvenile literature, every book for older children was supposed to instruct as well as amuse. And even when a story was supposedly just for fun, the fiction usually turned out to be little more than an excuse to admonish young readers to wash their faces, say their prayers, and keep their clothes clean. But gradually juvenile literature broke down into two categories, one for facts and one for fun. Gradually, too, the stiff, moralistic dramas thought proper for young readers gave way to real-life situations. No longer did a goody-goody such as Little Lord Fauntleroy square off against the forces of evil in the person of some dirty little urchin to drive home the point that cleanliness is next to godliness. Instead, readers were presented with a recognizable child who got homesick at boarding school, loved his dog, and had crushes on girls. He was even permitted to play tricks on his teachers and soil his clothes without being considered wicked.

In time publishers developed specialized categories of books to cater to the varying tastes of young readers. Thus, they put out romances especially for the teenage girl and adventure stories just for her younger brother. Americans had blazed the adventure trail with James Fenimore Cooper's exciting tales of Redskins and Palefaces on the frontier. Although not written for children, *The Last of the Mohicans* and his other novels "split the seams of the normal children's book" wide open, in the words of one authority. From Athens to Dublin to Philadelphia, children were soon shouting wild war whoops and taking aim at one another from behind large rocks. Children devoured anything about cowboys and Indians, and a minor literary industry was started which is still going strong 125 years later.

Magazines for children date from 1751 when John Newbery produced *The Lilliputian Magazine*. It was followed by a few others, but most of these early efforts were rather drab moralizing tracts rather than vehicles for entertainment. As time went on, though, children's magazines grew in number until, by the end of the nineteenth century, there was a bewildering assortment to choose from. The monthlies also became far more enjoyable as their articles were interspersed with foldout maps, sheet music, and a great many illustrations. In America the most famous children's magazine was *St. Nicholas*. As its editor stated her philosophy in its first issue in 1873: "Let there be no sermonizing . . . no spinning out of facts, no rattling of dry bones. . . . The ideal child's magazine is a pleasure ground." And the outstanding writers and artists who contributed to *St. Nicholas* did indeed make it a "pleasure ground" for generations of young readers.

In the nineteenth century children's magazines generally

cost a penny. Another kind of paperbound reading intended for youngsters, especially teenagers, cost the same sum. This was the "penny dreadful" or "blood" of Victorian England. For a penny children could indulge their love of bloodcurdling dangers, hair's-breadth escapes, and Robin Hood–type heroes. From their titles alone we can hear the screams and groans of *Varney the Vampire, The Castle Fiend, Geralda the Demon Nun* and *Almira's Curse.* Children read the penny dreadfuls avidly and uncritically, the way they would later immerse themselves in comic books. And publishers saw to it that they were well supplied. By the 1890s there were fifty or more new titles to chose from each week.

But not all the cheap soft-cover editions were junk. There were also penny-a-copy versions of fairy tales, travel books, and easy-to-read editions of the classics. Thanks to a new awareness of childhood, compulsory education laws, and the wonders of mass production, children could read widely for their own pleasure at last.

HEALTH

There was a close connection between the growing awareness of the child and an interest in his health. When the child moved out of the twilight zone between existence and nonexistence which he had occupied throughout history, his well-being took on great importance. The letters of General de Martagne, written between 1760 and 1780, show just how important. When he was away from home the General told his wife, "I should be so unhappy if I had no news about your health and that of my little girls." And on another occasion he wrote her: "I am not very happy about what you tell me about our little boy's pains and loss of appetite. I cannot recommend you too earnestly, dear child, to procure some Narbonne honey for both him and Xaviere, and to rub their gums with it when they are in pain." Before this an important military officer would never have concerned himself with such a trivial matter as teething.

Clinical pediatricians identified more and more diseases as the eighteenth century wore on. Gone were the elegant but inaccurate theories of the ancients; pediatricians now based their conclusions on first-hand observation. They were aided in this by the opening of lying-in hospitals and dispensaries just for children. One attending physician in George Armstrong's London dispensary, which treated thirty-five thousand children in its twelve-year existence, called for instruction in childhood diseases as part of regular medical training. The first British and American hospitals exclusively for children opened their doors just after 1850.

Smallpox was the greatest killer of all age groups in the eighteenth century, and it was a commonly accepted rule of thumb that a mother did not count her children until they had had—and survived—the disease. Various methods of protection against smallpox were introduced during the century, and parents weighed their pros and cons as they would later debate different means of preventing polio. General de Martagne advised his wife: "I leave it to you to see to Xaviere's vaccination, and the sooner the better, because everybody is satisfied with the vaccination." Jenner's method, by far the most effective, was announced in 1798. It was made compulsory in some European countries a mere nine years later.

There was also a new scientific approach to infant nutrition. Medical men had always been concerned about the quality of breast milk, but for the past twelve hundred years, their theories were little more than variations on the guidelines set down by the ancient writer Soranus in his celebrated nail test. Then in 1799 Englishman Michael Underwood included a detailed chemical analysis of milk on the flyleaf of his pediatric textbook. Underwood's analysis is considered a milestone in the history of human nutrition. Less than a hundred years later the Frenchman Louis Pasteur discovered how to destroy harmful bacteria through heating. This process, called pasteurization, guaranteed children safe milk, the first of its kind aside from human breast milk.

But perhaps the greatest aid of all to the child's physical well-being was the new field of hygiene. One of the pioneers in this area of preventive medicine was Dr. Joseph Clarke. Dr. Clarke studied the high incidence of tetanus or lockjaw among newborns in one of Ireland's new maternity hospitals. He came to the conclusion that it was due to lack of adequate ventilation. Although his diagnosis was faulty, many of the hygienic remedies he advocated removed the real cause of the disease: filth. In time Dr. Clarke's reforms cut down by two-thirds his hospital's infant mortality rate from the "nine-day fits," as tetanus was also called. The new appreciation of cleanliness and fresh air he helped to foster, coupled with improved nutrition, led to a dramatic decline in the mortality rate of children under five.

Eager to spread the word about recent developments in child health care—and their own theories, of course—European doctors began to produce a veritable avalanche of pediatric literature. They wrote textbooks and scholarly tracts for professional colleagues and popular books of advice for mothers. One of the most widely read doctors of the late eighteenth century was Englishman William Cadogan, who is called the father of pediatrics. Cadogan was against the overclothing and overfeeding of children, then common, and the use of "Mamby Pamby Stile" when speaking to them. He dispensed sensible advice on the whole, advice which coincides with modern child-rearing practices. All previous authorities had recommended feeding a baby on demand, but Cadogan came out in favor of regularized feeding schedules. And, in view of the high mortality rate for artificially fed infants, he vigorously recommended breast-feeding. Apparently some of his readers thought his advice about clothing was as crucial as that about breast-feeding, if we are to judge from this anecdote of his:

> A lady of great sway among her acquaintance told me not long ago with an air of reproach, that she had nursed her Child according to my book, and it died. I asked, if she had suckled it herself? No. Had it sucked any other woman? It was dry-nursed. Then, Madam, you cannot impute your misfortune to my advice,

for you have taken a method quite contrary to it, in the most capital point. Oh but, according to my direction, it had never worn stockings. Madam, Children may die, though they do or do not wear stockings.

WELFARE

Foundling hospitals had a long history on the Continent, going back to the orphanage of Datheus in medieval times. In 1421 the famous Ospedale degli Innocenti was founded in Florence, Italy, by the silk guild to take in that city's *gittatelli* or "castaways." Two hundred years later Vincent de Paul, patron saint of orphans, started a similar institution in Paris. But the sporadic attempts to organize a major foundling hospital in England never got off the ground.

Then, in the early eighteenth century, Captain Thomas Coram returned to England after a lengthy stay abroad. Appalled by the sight of dead and dying infants on the streets of London, he began to wage a campaign to give them a refuge. It took him seventeen years to attain his goal of establishing the London Foundling Hospital. It was an uphill battle, because the public was still more concerned with punishing the guilty mother than helping her innocent offspring, as this piece of criticism shows:

> The Hospital Foundling came out of the Brains,
> To encourage the progress of vulgar amours,
> The breeding of Rogues and the increasing of whores.
> While the children of honest and good husbands and wives,
> Stand exposed to oppression and want all their lives.

Ironically, European foundling hospitals were *too* successful. Swamped by tens of thousands of infants for whom they had neither the space nor the staff, they were unable to give them proper care. As a result, the mortality rate in these institutions soared as high as 80 percent. One contemporary writer called them a sure way to check population growth. But over time authorities learned how to manage foundling hospitals properly, and they went on to perform a much-needed service in an age when no satisfactory birth-control measures were known.

It was not an accident that the London Foundling Hospital was established at the same time that Newbery began publishing books for children, Rousseau was writing *Émile,* and pediatrics was becoming a legitimate branch of medicine. All these events stemmed from the same source: a growing concern for the happiness and welfare of children that, in turn, was part of a new humanitarian spirit in society. In Great Britain this could be seen in fairer trial procedures, a vigorous antislavery movement, and the establishment of organizations such as the Society for the Prevention of Cruelty to Animals. Ironically, animal protection societies were the first to take in abused children, and for a time some societies were serving two- and four-legged creatures simultaneously.

CHILD LABOR

Chained, belted, harnessed like dogs in a go-cart, black, saturated with wet, and more than half-naked— crawling upon their hands and feet, and dragging their heavy loads behind them—they present an appearance undescribably disgusting and unnatural.
—Commission on the Employment of Young Persons and
Children, 1842

The new humanitarian spirit was most aroused by the plight of children enmeshed in the Industrial Revolution, which started in England in the mid–eighteenth century.* Children had worked throughout history, but they did so in a home and

---

*Although the Industrial Revolution eventually spread to America and the continent of Europe, we shall focus on it in England, where the willingness of adults to exploit children can most clearly be seen.

family setting and were often outdoors in the fresh air. Where they did work inside, as apprentices, they were protected by guild rules and were taught a valuable trade. Now they had no such compensating niceties. The Industrial Revolution demanded great quantities of cheap labor which women and children alone could supply, and no particular care was taken for their well-being.

The earliest form of child labor to arouse the indignation of reformers was that of the chimney sweepers. In 1788 Parliament passed a law prohibiting the use of children under eight for this dangerous work, but a quarter of a century later a Parliamentary committee found that children as young as four were so employed. The committee reported that in order to get the children to climb into the narrow flues, some not more than seven inches square, "pins are forced into their feet by the boy that follows them up the chimney, in order to compel them to ascend it, and that lighted straw has been applied for that purpose." One witness testified that he had often been shut up in a long, narrow flue for six hours until he completed his work and was allowed to come out.

If some children risked losing their lives in this work, all risked losing their health. Their soft bones grew deformed from the pressure of standing long hours in awkward positions and from hauling twenty-five-pound bags of soot long distances. The children were also prey to a horrible disease called the chimney sweeper's cancer. If the children survived this hazardous work, they got no thanks for it. When they grew too large to be useful anymore, they were simply turned out onto the street with no education and no skills with which to earn a living. Little wonder that the chimney sweeper became the symbol of all that was evil in the Industrial Revolution.

Unbelievable as it seems, some of the chimney sweepers had been consigned to their lot by overburdened parents, and others were employed by their own fathers. But many of the children who suffered the worst abuses of industrialization were orphans. Inmates of England's poorhouses, they were indentured from the age of seven to the age of twenty-one— virtually without pay—to the new textile mills that were going up in different parts of the country.

Far from the sight of inspectors, the children were crammed into bare barracks, fifty to a room, and fed on such poor rations that they raided pigsties in order to get more food. Cruel overseers kept them at their machines for sixteen hours a day and countered any sign of slacking with severe beatings. The factory owners took few precautions to safeguard their little workers, so it was the rare child who survived his indenture without losing a finger, a hand, or even a whole limb. As a result of the excessive toil and lack of food, some children took sick, others became incurably lame. But the sick ones received no special rations except some sweetened water and no medical attention until they were dying.

Of course there was no place for education amid this unending drudgery. A law report of 1850 shows just how limited was the poor child's world:

ALDERMAN HUMPHREY: Do you know what an oath is?
BOY: No.
ALDERMAN: Can you read?
BOY: No.
ALDERMAN: Do you ever say your prayers?
BOY: No.
ALDERMAN: Do you know what prayers are?
BOY: No.
ALDERMAN: Do you know what God is?
BOY: No. . . .
ALDERMAN: What do you know?
BOY: I knows how to sweep a crossing.
ALDERMAN: And that's all?
BOY: That's all. I sweeps a crossing.

Charles Dickens used the foregoing conversation almost word for word in *Bleak House.* In that novel, *Oliver Twist,* and his other books, he kept hammering away at the exploitation of poor children. Dickens knew firsthand the horrors of industrial life, for he himself had been an apprentice in a blacking factory at the age of ten. With the great leader Benjamin Disraeli and others in England, he used his literary talents to make the public aware of these abuses and to effect reforms. In France Victor Hugo was trying to accomplish the same thing. His novel *les Misérables* laid bare the evils of baby farming and the horrible lot of poor children in general, while *l'Homme qui rit* exposed the vicious practice of disfiguring destitute orphans to make them more successful beggars.

REFORM

Although the public sympathized with the children's plight, reform was not easy to accomplish. The mill and mine owners were making too great a profit on the labor of their docile little workers to give them up without a struggle.

The opening rounds of the battle for reform took place in Manchester, England. Manchester was the leading cotton center in the world and it was here that the worst abuses of the early Industrial Revolution were to be found. Starting in 1784 the magistrates of that city tried to prohibit mill owners from working their juvenile employees more than ten hours a day or during the night. But more than a decade later neither of these requirements had been met. The controversy over conditions in Manchester led Sir Robert Peel to sponsor the Factory Act of 1802. This act, which was limited to apprentice children who were orphaned wards of the state, set a twelve-hour work limit in textile mills and required some hygienic measures as well as some provision for schooling. Although nothing came of it because no money was provided to enforce it, the Factory Act of 1802 deserves an important place in history. It was the first piece of social legislation to result from the Industrial Revolution and the first to insure the well-being of citizens just because they were young.

Sir Robert Peel did not give up. With other reformers, he worked for the passage of more laws to protect child laborers. He got the laws passed—but never with any real means of enforcement. When Parliament held hearings in 1832 for yet another law, the manufacturers organized to oppose it. They bribed witnesses, physicians among them, to testify that even a twenty-three-hour work day was not too much for a child! Despite this testimony, Parliament passed a law prohibiting children under nine from working in the textile mills and limiting the hours for children above thirteen to twelve hours a day. This time inspection was provided for. Yet the manufacturers still balked, and it took some years before this law was fully operative.

The reformers did not look upon the Factory Act of 1833 as the end of their battle. They had their sights set on a ten-hour day and the elimination of all child labor in the mines. In 1842 Lord Shaftsbury headed the Commission on the Employment of Young Persons and Children. The Commission heard from the children themselves what it was like to spend hours at a time, alone, in the bowels of the earth just to earn a few pennies. Some of the workers who endured this hideous punishment—for which they had committed no crime except that of being poor—were boys and girls five years of age. Here is the testimony of a child of eight:

I'm a trapper in the Gamber pit. I have to trap without a light, and I'm scared. I never go to sleep. Sometimes I sing when I've a light, but not in the dark; I dare not sing then.

Lord Shaftsbury's report so shocked the English people that Parliament prohibited the mine owners from ever sending either women or children underground again. Five years later Parliament passed the Ten Hour Act, which had the effect of making the ten-hour day the norm in all industries. Yet abuses continued, necessitating still more hearings and more laws. Only with the Factory Act of 1874 did the British people feel that they had dealt adequately with the problem of child labor.

THE VICTORIAN CHILD

The enormous sympathy aroused by the plight of the working child was both a sign and a cause of the child's newly important status. The child had come into his own. It is ironical, though, that this first true recognition led not to his emancipation but to his separation from society. This was due in no small measure to the times in which the child came to the fore. The nineteenth century—the Victorian era—was stiff, sentimental, prudish, and, in some ways, very brutal.

For generations family members had observed a code of formality in dealing with one another in upper-class British and French homes. Indeed, displays of affection were considered the height of bad taste on both sides of the English Channel. Then, changes in French society after the Revolution of 1789 led to warmer relations between parents and children there. In Great Britain, on the other hand, the aristocratic coldness toward children grew more widespread, filtering down to the middle classes in the Victorian era.

Although nineteenth-century child-rearing manuals urged closer maternal ties, many English mothers seemed to have been cool and distant. Harriet Martineau recalled that her mother so rarely hugged her that when a stranger happened to pet her, she burst into tears. Winston Churchill and other Victorian children so seldom saw their mothers that they looked upon them as special, glamorous guests. Fathers were, if anything, more remote. Austin Harrison remembered that his father's presence was a ceremonial in which the older man seemed always to be on a pedestal. There was no easy conversational give and take, because "Respect was the injunction of the family; sons kept their distance and looked up." Not for nothing was the patriarchal Victorian father called "the Governor."

One important reason why parents and children found it so difficult to talk to one another was that they led totally separate existences. Parents spent all their time in business and social settings. Children spent all their time away at school or sequestered in day and night nurseries. They were only summoned to appear before their parents at a set hour of the day. Care of the children was entrusted to a nanny, a kind of bathing and supervising nurse who was usually unmarried and very proper. Far from being the jolly Mary Poppins depicted on film, many nannies were strict to the point of being sadistic. Others could be warm and maternal, however, providing most of the love in a Victorian child's life.

The regimen in the nursery was often severe, consisting of ice-cold baths and simple, monotonous meals. Rich food was not served to children because it was considered bad for their digestion and morals. Yet despite the nursery's austere aspects, many adults looked back on it fondly. They recalled with pleasure the long, unstructured afternoons in which they were free to read, put on puppet shows, challenge one of their numerous siblings to a board game, or play with some of the wonderful toys that filled the nursery cupboards. In addition to the old favorites such as rocking horses, hoops, marbles, and soldiers, Victorian children delighted in the steam-driven train sets that were introduced during this era. They also indulged a passion for bell-ringing toys, wheel-mounted toys, and jack-in-the-boxes. Dolls were probably never more beautiful and, after the baby doll was introduced to England in 1825, probably never more beloved than at this time. Victorian dolls were often equipped with houses, carriages, numerous changes of clothing, and every personal accessory known to man including miniature watches and tiny hot water bottles.

Given the great quantity of clothing they had to wear, it is a wonder that these children could play with toys at all. From the day a Victorian girl could walk she was loaded down with a vest, a chemise, a corset stiffened with whalebone strips or "stays," drawers, black stockings held up with garters, a flannel petticoat, a white petticoat with a bodice, a dress, and, finally, a pinafore! Little boys were also burdened with all this paraphernalia, but at the age of seven or so they were "breeched." Walter de la Mare commemorated this great day in his collection, *Early One Morning in the Spring:*

> Joy to Philip! he this day
> Has his long coats cast away,
> And, (the childish season gone)
> Puts the manly breeches on . . .
> Sashes, frocks to those that need 'em.
> Philip's limbs have got their freedom.
> He can run, or he can ride,
> And do twenty things beside
> Which his petticoats forbad:
> Is he not a happy lad?

SENTIMENTALITY VERSUS BRUTALITY

Ever since the Romantics had discovered—if not created—the child, he had been used to symbolize Nature, Imagination, and Innocence. With industrialization and its emphasis on acquiring money, the child increasingly became a symbol also of humanity versus the machine. The Romantics had used the child as a vigorous image of life—life at the glorious moment of its unfolding. But Victorian writers used him for something quite different—the creation of sentimental pathos. Instead of celebrating the child's vigor, they emphasized his frailty. And in a society gone mad with the pursuit of wealth, how could such a weak reed survive, much less triumph? There was only one literary solution, it seemed—the sickness or premature death of a central childhood character.

The writer who did more than any other to popularize this sentimental approach to childhood was Charles Dickens. He moved England to tears over the deaths of Paul Dombey and Little Nell and the crippling affliction of Tiny Tim. Dickens created many memorable child characters and, with *Oliver Twist,* he made the child the true center of fictional interest for the first time in English literature. *Oliver Twist* is remarkable, indeed, for its accurate account of the world as seen through a child's eyes. But with Dickens that world was always oppressive, the child always helpless to defend himself against it.

While Victorian writers sentimentalized childhood, they also used it as a symbol of escape. Increasingly disillusioned with their restrictive, pressured society, many Victorian writers embarked upon a literary quest to regain the unregainable—the irresponsibility of youth. George Eliot was one of the first to speak with nostalgia of childhood's "golden gates" and its "daisied fields." Other writers joined in, creating a state of childhood as unrealistically perfect as it was unobtainable. This cult of nostalgia culminated in the stage appearance of British writer J. M. Barrie's supreme creation, Peter Pan. Peter Pan was a boy who would not grow up. He lived with other little boys on a never-never land of the always young. Obviously, Peter Pan answered a deep longing for escape in the Victorian heart, for he became a cult in his own right. His popularity was astounding. As Barrie's biographer described it: "Hundreds and thousands of [adults] at all kinds of extraordinary ages, fell right into his open trap. . . . They couldn't get away from it. And they, too, suddenly hated being grown up."

But while they were shedding copious tears over fictional children "gone to a fairer world than this" and signing petitions to improve the lot of poor children in factories and slums, Victorians were abusing children right in their own "respectable" homes. And they were doing so with the tacit approval of the whole society. The French had long since dropped flogging in their schools and harsh beatings in their homes. By the 1840s

Britons in child-rearing manuals were urging their countrymen to do the same. But from the evidence of memoirs and fictionalized autobiographies, Victorian boys and girls were still subject to frequent harsh beatings in addition to being locked up and deprived of food for even the most minor misdemeanors. As Samuel Butler described the situation in *The Way of All Flesh:*

> Mr. Pontifex may have been a little sterner with his children than some of his neighbours, but not much. He thrashed his boys two or three times a week and some weeks a good deal oftener, but in those days fathers were always thrashing their boys. . . . St. Paul had placed disobedience to parents in very ugly company. . . .

One common reason for punishment was any expression of interest in sex, no matter how innocent, because the Victorians clung fiercely to the notion of childhood purity. They bore down on anything that seemed to contradict or threaten it. Thus, some adults closely examined juvenile reading matter for moral content. They banned some books outright and cleaned up others for childish consumption. As we have seen, the Victorians made sure that children covered up every part of themselves with clothing, a practice they followed, too. But perhaps most damaging of all, they made children feel guilty about indulging a perfectly natural curiosity about their bodies. The Victorians were particularly horrified by masturbation or "self-abuse," which they termed the cardinal sin of childhood. To prevent it they tied down wandering hands at night and meted out even more severe punishment to habitual offenders.

Parents brought other pressures to bear on their children by reminding them of their duty to increase the family fortune through hard work and the "right" marriage. Though children might have been—and, we now know, often were—seething with hatred toward their repressive fathers, they had to pay them extravagant forms of deference at all times. They also had to meet impossible standards of good conduct—at all times.

Even on his sickbed, Samuel Butler's little Ernest Pontifex was not let off the hook: "His mamma had told him he need not be afraid of dying, for he would go straight to heaven, if he would only be sorry for having done his lessons so badly and vexed his poor papa."

Finally, it became too much—the sexual guilt, the harsh punishments, the unrealistic expectations of good conduct. Children began to crack under the pressure. One indication of the tensions seething beneath the smooth exterior of Victorian family life was the sharp increase in child suicides in the 1890s. Contemporary studies cited shame, fear of punishment, and misery of family life as the chief causes of this phenomenon.

Officially, the Victorian era came to an end in 1901. But the child continued to live within its thrall for many, many years thereafter. Only Freud's startling revelations about childhood sexuality, two world wars, and America's liberating influence finally freed the child from the protective, one might say suffocating, cocoon of Victorian England.

CHAPTER SIX

A NEW CHILD
FOR A NEW LAND

Although childhood continued to evolve in Europe, after 1900 most major trends affecting this stage of life originated in America. Therefore, we shall now shift the focus of our inquiry to this side of the Atlantic. We cannot just pick up our story where we left off in post-Victorian times, however. To understand twentieth-century American childhood, we must first understand seventeenth-, eighteenth-, and nineteenth-century American childhood. It is well that we've studied European history, too, because far from being something totally new under the sun, the American child has been shaped in large measure by his European antecedents.

SOMETHING OLD . . .

In crossing the Atlantic, the colonists did not instantly become new men. They brought much of the Old World with them: their household goods, their clothing, their religious beliefs— and their child-rearing practices. Like European children of the time, colonial babies were breast-fed on demand, pacified with cordials, infrequently bathed, and "taught" how to walk in go-carts and standing stools.

Like their European counterparts, too, colonial children were susceptible to smallpox, diptheria, and other diseases. They were given the same exotic potions and were alternately sweated and bled. From the high juvenile death rate we can

Here, three children listen intently to "Contes de Ma Mere Loye" or Mother Goose stories. The fireside was a common spot for storytelling. (The Pierpont Morgan Library.)

An example of John Newbery's enjoyable approach to publishing books for children. (The Pierpont Morgan Library.)

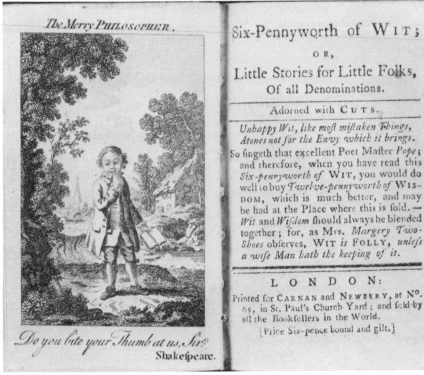

The Merry Philosopher.

Do you bite your Thumb at us, Sir?
Shakespeare.

Six-Pennyworth of W I T ;

O R,

Little Stories for Little Folks,
Of all Denominations.

Adorned with C U T S.

Unhappy Wit, like most mistaken Things,
Atones not for the Envy which it brings.
So singeth that excellent Poet Master *Pope*;
and therefore, when you have read this
Six-pennyworth of W I T, you would do
well to buy *Twelve-pennyworth of* W I S-
DOM, which is much better, and may
be had at the Place where this is sold. —
Wit and *Wisdom* should always be blended
together; for, as Mrs. *Margery Two-*
Shoes observes, W I T *is* F O L L Y, *unless*
a wise Man hath the keeping of it.

L O N D O N:

Printed for CARNAN and NEWBERY, at Nº.
65, in St. Paul's Church-Yard; and sold by
all the Booksellers in the World.
[Price Six-pence bound and gilt.]

This mid-eighteenth-century classroom was better equipped than most, because it had a globe and a map. Apparently, it also came equipped with a dunce cap for the poor soul who could not recite his lesson properly. (Museum of the City of New York.)

Children who lived in the early nineteenth century were always being warned about the consequences of disobedience. (The Pierpont Morgan Library.)

V.

The giddy Girl.

MISS HELEN was always too giddy to heed
    What her mother had told her to shun;
For frequently over the street, in full speed,
    She would cross where the carriages run.

And out she would go, to a very deep well,
    To look at the water below;
How naughty! to run to a dangerous well,
    Where her mother forbade her to go!

One morning, intending to take but one peep,
    Her foot slipp'd away from the ground;
Unhappy misfortune! the water was deep,
    And giddy Miss Helen was drown'd.

A 7

Children have always played by imitating their parents' work. (New York State Historical Association, Cooperstown.)

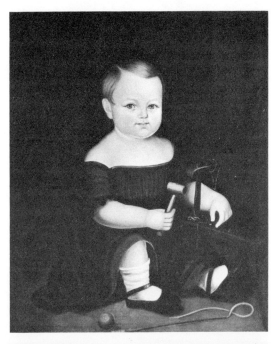

This is the ideal Victorian family scene: the paterfamilias surrounded by his wife and children of various ages. It leaves no doubt as to who ruled the roost. (Museum of the City of New York.)

These upper-class children of the late Victorian era are enjoying the scrapbooks and magazines then being published in profusion for young people. (Museum of the City of New York.)

The passion for dollhouses and miniature furnishings reached its peak in Victorian times. (Museum of the City of New York.)

assume that these "cures" were no more effective in the New World than they had been in the Old. The Puritans were supposedly fatalistic about death, because original sin was thought to be the ultimate cause of all illness. Yet they embraced vaccination in order to save their children from the scourge of smallpox. By the eighteenth century colonial parents were exhibiting that concern over physical well-being that characterized European family life at the same time. Thus, we read in a letter from a Boston minister to his nine-year-old daughter: "Take care of your health and as you love me do not eat green apples. Drink sparingly of water, except the day be warm."

European habits of dress also crossed the ocean, which meant that children wore the same styles as their parents. Among pious Puritans and Quakers and the poor, these clothes were usually made of plain homespun. But among the less religious and the wealthy, the sky was the limit. As was the custom in Europe, children of the rich were dressed in elaborate velvet and satin costumes which were augmented on special occasions with precious jewelry, masks, and fans. Boys as young as seven wore expensive wigs.

European habits of play—and the articles of play themselves—were transported to the New World, too. In William Penn's baggage when he came to Pennsylvania, for example, was a wooden doll with slant eyes and an oval face. What they didn't bring with them, the colonists often imported. In 1712 "Boxes of Toys" were among the cargo of a ship putting into Boston Harbor and in 1743 the *Boston News Letter* advertised "Dutch and English Toys for Children." From Germany came elaborate pull toys and from the Far East strange, brightly colored coaches and other exotic items for children. The *Pennsylvania Packet* carried an advertisement by a London cabinetmaker stating that "he makes Rocking-Horses in the neatest and best manner, to teach children to ride and give them a whole-some and pleasing exercise."

When it was too expensive or inconvenient to import a toy, colonial fathers were set to work making it themselves. They fashioned doll-sized cradles and other miniature furniture and whittled pull toys in the shape of every known animal, but especially the horse. They made dolls out of wood called "pennywoods" or "peg dolls" and dolls made out of corn husks. But the ones parents made most often, and the only one seen by many colonial children, was the rag doll. It consisted of linen or unbleached cotton that was stuffed with sawdust and decorated with a painted face.

Colonial children spent even more time on games than on toys. As if by magic, all the old European favorites turned up in America intact: "Scotch-hoppers," tag, kite flying, blindman's buff, leapfrog, stool ball, backgammon, checkers, chess, cards, dice—the list goes on and on. Many of these games date back to medieval times; most are still being played. For example, "Here We Go Round the Mulberry Bush" and "London Bridge Is Falling Down" were as familiar to tots three hundred years ago as they are today.

In addition to the universally popular games, each nationality brought over its own particular amusements. For example, the Dutch were fond of bowling on greens, sledding, and ice skating. The Puritans had taken to skating while in Holland, their home for several years after fleeing England, and they continued to enjoy this form of relaxation after moving on to the New World. On the last day of November, 1696, Judge Sewell recorded in his diary that many scholars went to "scate" on Fresh Pond. Alas, they did not test the ice first and two boys named Maxwell and Eyre fell in and were drowned.

But from Europe, too, came the firm belief that children should be diligent. Thus, some of the activities we do for fun, colonial children did for a purpose. The best example of this is the sampler, which every little girl, rich or poor, was expected to make. The sampler was a piece of cloth on which a girl practiced her sewing by copying the alphabet, often in cross-stitch. Making a sampler was considered a valuable pastime because, in addition to improving a girl's skill, it taught her the alphabet and encouraged perseverance and neatness. As a girl became more skillful, she often embellished the cloth with embroidered fruits and flowers and stiff little figures representing angels, shepherds, and animals. Some samplers were true works of art.

. . . SOMETHING NEW

The European ways, then, came over with the pots and pans and dolls and hoes. But many of them did not remain European for long. The new environment worked on the old values, the old ways of doing things, the old family relationships until they were almost unrecognizable. In time everyone agreed that something new had been created, something they called "American."

From the beginning the New World was supposed to be a better world. Something in the air here was going to improve everything and everyone, especially the children. This expectation was deliberately exploited by the propaganda literature circulated throughout Europe to encourage immigration. It depicted America as a healthful place in which to bring up children, a theme frequently sounded in private letters, too. A typical piece of puffery by a new settler declared:

> The Christian children born here are generally well-favored and beautiful to behold. I never knew any to come into the world with the least blemish on any part of the body; being in the general observed to be better-natured, milder, and more tender-hearted than those born in England.

Perhaps because they were expected to be different, colonial children *were* different. They seemed more precocious, more adaptable, more adventurous, and more self-assured than their European counterparts. In 1685 Cotton Mather, the first man on record to use the term "American," observed, "The Youth in this Country are verie Sharp and early Ripe in their Capacities."

To a great extent American parents encouraged this independence. A visitor to upstate New York noted that children of Dutch descent were "permitted to range about at full liberty in their earliest years." American parents sent boys and girls to the same elementary schools and in later years let them go about together unchaperoned, a custom which shocked many visitors from abroad. Parents also encouraged children to put their best foot forward socially. In Europe children were required to hang back; here they were told to speak up. As the Boston minister told his daughter: "When I last saw you, you were too shame-faced; look people in the face, speak freely and behave decently. . . ." And a Swedish traveler in Pennsylvania reported that "It is nothing uncommon to see little children giving sprightly and ready answers to questions that are proposed to them. . . ."

But not everyone applauded this precocity. To some it was impudence, not independence. And, by all accounts, American children were harder to handle than those on the other side. They did not have the ancient institutions and the unquestioning belief in obedience that kept European children in line. Moreover, there *was* something in the air here and that something was liberty. It encouraged adults to defy authority and it encouraged their children—ironically—to defy them. As Richard Hall's grandmother, with whom he boarded, complained:

> Richard wears out nigh 12 paire of shoes a year. He brought 12 hankers with him and they have all been lost long ago; and I have bought him 3 or 4 more at a time. His way is to tie knottys at one end & beat ye Boys with them and then to lose them and *he cares not a bit what I will say to him* [italics added].

To be sure, there was a great deal of talk about discipline.

Sermons on the subject abounded. But the new land was too vast, the chores too numerous to keep a vigil over children's activities. And in the new country father did not always know best. Unhampered by a traditional upbringing, his children were often better at adapting to the quick-changing American scene than he.

Thus, relations between the generations were bound to be strained in America. Time and again European ideas of obedience clashed with American conditions of liberty, and time and again obedience lost. Nowhere was this struggle more acute than among the Puritans, who based their entire future on the young members of their group.

GREAT EXPECTATIONS

I pray consider, what was the thing proposed? why came you into this land? was it not mainly with respect to the rising Generation? *And what with respect to them? was it to leave them a rich and wealthy people? was it to leave them Houses, Lands, Livings? Oh no: but to leave God in the midst of them.*
—Eleazer Mather, to the older generation

Although Puritans were supposed to love God above any mortal creature, they assumed that parents "naturally" loved their children. This love was not supposed to be displayed through too much overt affection, however, nor were children to be treated as equals. A "due distance" was advised by one of the founding fathers because "fondness and familiarity breeds and causeth contempt and irreverence in children." In part it was this fear of spoiling their children that frequently led the Puritans to send them to the homes of relatives, friends, and even total strangers. Like their European counterparts, the children thus "put out" usually became servants for a time.

For their part, children had a "duty" to love their parents. The children's attitude was supposed to be one of reverence, an affection mixed with fear. They were not supposed to seem too familiar or assuming, nor, above all, were they ever to disobey. The Puritans' conscience, the great Protestant leader John Calvin, himself had said: "Those who violate the parental authority by contempt or rebellion are not men but monsters. Therefore the Lord commands all those who are disobedient to their parents to be put to death."

Children were never put to death on these grounds in New England. Nor does it seem that they were even punished more harshly, more frequently, or for lesser offenses than children today. Of course the Puritans were greatly concerned with obedience—but they demanded it as much of adults as of children.

Parents preferred to develop internal controls in their children. Although fiery minister Cotton Mather's injunction "Better whipt, than Damn'd" was undoubtedly followed, external force was a last resort. Mather himself was sparing of physical punishment. "I would never come to give a child a Blow; except in Case of Obstinacy: or some gross Enormity," he wrote. "To be chased for a while out of my Presence, I would make to be look'd upon as the Sorest Punnishment in the Family."

Keeping their children on the path of righteousness was of critical importance to the Puritans. Indeed, though they left the Old World for a variety of reasons, the one they talked about most was fleeing its corruption for the sake of the children. "We did it all for you" became an article of faith among them. Ministers particularly liked this theme, because it reminded the older generation of its duty to make children toe the line and it impressed upon the younger generation its responsibility to carry on the true religion. As Increase Mather exhorted the younger members of the flock, "It was for your sakes especially, that your Fathers ventured their lives upon the rude waves of the vast Ocean. . . . that they might train up a Generation for Christ."

But the environment was not conducive to keeping the Puritan strain pure in terms of either bloodlines or behavior, because as many as eight out of ten early arrivals in Massachusetts Bay were not church members or "saints." Thus, even though the Puritans controlled the government and set the standards of behavior, their children were still exposed to corrupting influences. Their ministers soon began to rail against bad company in New England as feverishly as they had in old England. One of them, Josiah Smith, urged parents to keep their children at home, because "the times are so degenerate that 'tis hardly safe to trust them anywhere, from your own inspection and care without danger to their morals."

Parents urged, ministers preached and threatened, but it was a losing battle. Puritan children could not seem to develop the same special relationship with God that their parents had, and by 1700 the Puritan system was on its last legs. Why? Not because parents had loved their children too little, but because they had loved them too much. They had refused to look beyond them for new church members. The Puritans had interpreted "Love thy neighbor" as "Love thy family" and set their children above God in their affections, something they had always warned themselves not to do. Then, when the children couldn't deliver, they had nowhere else to turn. Cotton Mather's disillusionment with his own offspring symbolized the shattered dreams of the whole Puritan experiment in Christian living. "How little *Comfort,* yea, how much contrary to it, have I seen in my *Children?*" he commented ruefully.

SCHOOL DAYS

In colonial times "education" encompassed far more vocational and religious training than it does today, and almost all of it was transmitted through the home. Still, formal schooling did exist in colonial times from the beginning. Because of its contribution to salvation, the Puritans were particularly committed to the idea of formal education. In the words of one minister, "Unless school and college flourish, church and state cannot live."

The Puritans demonstrated the seriousness of their commitment by founding Harvard College in 1636, only six years after they arrived in Massachusetts Bay. No other colonizers had ever provided for higher education so quickly. Actually, it would have been simpler and cheaper to send the most promising young men back to England to study at one of the great British universities, but piety and pride dictated the establishment of a Puritan college on American soil to train up the next generation of ministers.

The founding of Harvard College was a remarkable achievement, but it did not stand alone. A Massachusetts Bay law of 1647 decreed that every town of fifty families or more had to provide a school where their children could learn to read, write, and do sums. Towns of one hundred families or more had to support a second master who was capable of teaching Latin and Greek. Parents could send their children to these schools or educate them at home as they wished, but the establishment of the schools was compulsory. In time every New England colony except Rhode Island mandated the building of schoolhouses and the education of children. With all the work to be done in the New World, these obligations were often slighted. Still, by 1700 nineteen out of twenty men in New England could sign their names, a high percentage for those days.

New England schools were public but not free. Parents were expected to contribute small sums, to cover part of the teacher's salary, and to provide logs for the school fireplace, an important item in those hard New England winters. Colonial schoolhouses were crude affairs, little more than log cabins at first. Since there was no glass for the windows, newsprint or white paper was greased with lard and tacked over holes in the walls to let in a dim light. Furnishings were spare—no blackboards, maps, globes, or any of the accessories we usually associate with learning. Into this barren room the children trooped at seven or eight in the morning, not to leave again until four or five in the afternoon, except for a two-hour break at noon. School was held six days a week with vacations at Christmas and midsummer.

Like their European counterparts, colonial children started out with a hornbook. The American version usually consisted of the alphabet in small and capital letters, combinations of consonants and vowels, the Exorcism and the Lord's Prayer. After this was mastered, the children moved on to a first reader or primer. The most popular primer of all time was *The New England Primer,* which is reputed to have sold an astounding six million copies in various editions. Like so many schoolbooks in those days, *The New England Primer* relied heavily on rhymes to aid memorization. Its famous opening stanzas show that even in teaching the ABCs, the Puritans could not resist preaching a moral:

> In *A*dam's fall
> We sinned all.

> Thy life to mend,
> God's *B*ook attend.

Both boys and girls learned to read a hornbook and master an elementary speller and perhaps a first reader. But all education beyond the three R's was almost exclusively reserved for boys, just as it was in Europe. According to Abigail Adams: "Female education in the best families, went no further than writing and arithmetic; in some rare instances music and dancing."

For most boys it did not go much further, either. Especially in the earlier years, only those boys who expected to attend college or pursue a learned profession enrolled in the grammar schools. In colonial times these took the place of our high schools, because the "grammar" of their title referred to Latin, the language of all scholarly texts. A boy entered a grammar school at the age of eight or so and spent seven years in its classes. Then, if he was bright enough and his father wealthy enough, he might go on to college.

By the time of the Revolution he had nine colleges to choose from. They had all been founded by Protestant sects and they offered theological study as well as all the classical subjects of the traditional European university on which they were patterned. Colonial colleges loudly proclaimed their high educational purpose and standards. Perhaps too loudly. From the evidence that we have, both administration and teachers seem to have spent much of their time and energy disciplining rowdy students; and many parents seem to have sent their hard-to-handle sons to college for the very purpose of this discipline. Even illustrious Harvard often had its hands full.

LOG CABINS AND OLD-FIELD SCHOOLS

The early country schoolhouses of New York and Pennsylvania were made of logs. They often had a dirt floor which could be readily ground up into thick clouds—especially when some mischievous boys wanted to annoy their schoolmaster with the dust. The master's desk was usually placed in the center of the room. The younger children sat on blocks or benches made of logs, facing him. The older students sat at rude plank desks extending from the wall, their backs to him.

A single master taught all the subjects in all the grades; only rarely did he have an assistant and then only in the larger towns. In the Middle and Southern Colonies schoolmasters were often indebted immigrants and exported convicts. Whether because of a sordid past, the miserable wages they were paid, or the prospect of facing a roomful of rambunctious children in the morning, many of them were frequently drunk. Scottish immigrants were supposedly the best of the lot.

Schoolhouses shaped like hexagons were a feature of education in the Middle Colonies. They were built by the Quakers, who felt that the three R's were sufficient for most people. They were wary of further education because, in their view, it fostered undue pride and provoked idleness. Their German neighbors in Pennsylvania were even less enthusiastic about education. They contended that schooling made boys dissatisfied with their lot on the farm and that religion suffered from too much learning. They built a few schools for the lower elementary grades, but they held indignant meetings and even filed suits to block attempts at establishing places of higher learning in their communities. Among the Dutch settlers of New Netherland, education was essentially in the hands of private teachers who were supervised, at least on paper, by the authorities.

Although nowhere outside of New England did governmental bodies actively encourage education, the situation in the South was even worse than in the Middle Colonies. Public elementary schools were few and far between there for most of the colonial period. Not until 1723, for example, did the Maryland assembly take the initial step of providing for a school in each of its counties. Secondary education in the South was even less well provided for, consisting of a handful of expensive schools in the region's few large towns. The founding of Virginia's College of William and Mary in 1693 provided Southerners with their first opportunity to obtain a higher education in their own region.

Wealthy Southern planters solved the problem of educating their children by importing tutors from the North or England or using an indentured servant for that purpose. Some Southern boys were taken into a minister's home to study, and a few offspring of the wealthiest families were sent abroad for their education. Still another solution was the cooperative venture. In Virginia, the Carolinas, and Georgia a few neighbors sometimes got together to hire a teacher. They set him up in a shabby building on an exhausted tobacco field and entrusted their children to his care.

George Washington got most of his education in just such an

"old-field school" from one Mr. Hobby, sexton, pedagogue, and "the most conceited man in three parishes." From some accounts, Washington was extraordinarily determined to get an education. One year he rode his horse ten miles each way to get to school and another year he rowed across the river—in rough weather as well as smooth—to study with a teacher in Fredericksburg. Washington had to give up his pursuit of a formal education at the age of thirteen, but by then he had filled in a tall stack of copybooks and acquired an excellent command of the English language.

Not all Southern children were endowed with Washington's academic drive. And, without a school close at hand, they simply went without. They were the victims of several circumstances, not the least of which was the region's low-density population pattern. The South simply did not have the village life of the North with which to support local schools. As a report to the Bishop of London concluded:

> This lack of schools in Virginia is a consequence of their scattered planting. It renders a very numerous generation of Christian's Children born in Virginia, who naturally are of beautiful and comely Persons, and generally of more ingenious Spirits than those in England, unserviceable for any great Employment in Church or State.

Some would have disagreed with this report, for the South turned out numerous soldiers and lawmakers who were most "serviceable" to the state. Patrick Henry defended the "naiteral parts" of his fellow Virginians, which, he said, were of more account than "all the book-lairnin' on the airth."

WHO NEEDS LATIN?

Patrick Henry put into words what many "practical people" felt during the colonial period—and what many "practical people" feel today. To them, education was and always will be a frill. Of course, on the frontier this anti-intellectual attitude was not unreasonable. A person did not need to know Latin to chop down a tree, and the time a child spent in school was time he lost to the fields. As they struggled to carve a home out of the wilderness, even the Puritans often failed to fulfill their educational obligations to their children.

Because of the widely held belief in practical knowledge, colleges were never central to colonial life. The classical courses they offered had no practical application and their degrees were not required for any career. Apprenticeship was the recognized form of "education" for most trades and even for the learned professions. If a young man wanted to become a doctor, for example, he attached himself to a practicing physician. He visited sick patients with the older man and then went home to pore over medical texts, memorize anatomical drawings, and try his hand at pounding pills. Would-be lawyers took much the same approach, clerking in the office of an established firm by day and reading the law by night.

For most of the colonial period, then, formal education was only a small and not very significant part of the whole learning process. But as the frontier struggle ended for many communities and a more complex, urbane way of life took its place, formal education was no longer considered such a frill. A college education still did not transmit useful skills, but it did confer the status which was increasingly needed to get ahead. Once poorly paid, college graduates started to get the best clients, the best patients, and the best pulpits. On the eve of the Revolution there were only three thousand living alumni of American colleges, but this group of men was influential far beyond what its small number would suggest.

Below the college level, too, formal schooling was becoming more and more important. At one time the home—backed up by a strong community and church—had been adequate to transmit all the values, book learning, and vocational training a child needed. But the church weakened and community ties loosened. Parents found themselves unequal to the task of teaching the skills necessary for life in a complex society. After the Revolution the public schools would increasingly take their place.

"BY THE SWEAT OF THY BROWS . . ."

Throughout the colonial period the child was not primarily a student because he was first and foremost a worker. This was not considered a social problem by the colonists; it was merely a social fact. In England people were accustomed to using small children around the house, farm, or shop, and they carried this custom with them across the Atlantic. Indeed, in the New World they relied on it more than ever.

The Puritans needed their children to help them clear the land, sow and harvest the crops, and build the barns. They needed them to help dry the cod, distill the rum, shoe the horses, and do all the hundreds of other things that needed doing in a new land. But the Puritans looked upon this child labor as more than a practical necessity. They *believed* in it as a righteous institution. They considered industriousness a virtue, idleness a sin; and their court records reveal many vigorous attempts to prevent the latter among the younger generation. Nor were they alone in this attitude. Pennsylvania Quakers also felt so strongly about the work ethic that they had their children write every day in their copybooks, "By the sweat of thy brows thou shalt eat thy bread."

The kind of work one did was so important to the Puritans that they named it the "calling." Nowadays, only the ministry is referred to that way, because it implies that God himself called a person to do His work in the world. But the Puritans felt that through labor a man *was* serving God. Since the calling was so important and so difficult to change later on, boys usually postponed the choice until they were anywhere from ten to fourteen years of age. Even then, the voice that "called" them to a profession was more likely that of their father than of the Divinity. Since the future of a little girl was almost certainly that of wife and mother, no real choice or training was involved. Therefore, girls sometimes apprenticed earlier than boys. Usually one boy in a family was designated to inherit the farm while the others sought their livelihood elsewhere.

Sometimes children continued to live at home during their apprenticeship, but more often they moved in with the master and his family. Then, for all practical purposes, the master became the "father" who was required to teach the apprentice how to read and how to ply a trade, just as he was required to teach his own children. The apprentice became the "son" who had to give the master respect and obedience, just as he had to obey his own father. But the relationship was not exactly familial, because the apprentice was still considered the master's property. The boy could not marry without his consent, vote, or engage in trade. Moreover, a common clause in the apprenticeship contract stated that he could not "absent himself day nor night from his Master's service without his leave," although in actuality this may not have been carried out fully.

In many cases master and apprentice developed a very close relationship. Some men virtually adopted their charges, others left them an inheritance in their wills, and some boys remembered their former teachers with affection all their lives. But things did not always work out this well. No guilds developed in the New World as they had in the Old to supply supervision. Without such a central authority to answer to and under the pressure of work, many masters let their educational obligations slide. The father-son aspects of the relationship faded, too, as colonists began to think of apprenticeship more as a kind of employment and less as a kind of education preparatory to employment. The apprentice came to be treated as just another hired hand.

WORK IS GOOD FOR YOU

From the community's point of view, apprenticing or binding out children served a variety of purposes. It was the way seventeenth-century towns took care of orphans, since there were no orphanages in the New World. It was also the way they got children of the poor off their relief or "welfare" rolls. Following English custom, the town of Boston instructed a number of indigent parents to bind out their children as indentured servants. If they failed to take this action, the town warned, "the selectmen will take their said children from them and place them with such masters as they shall provide according as the law directs." Some of the children in question were as young as eight.

Work was also used as a correctional device. Lacking jails, early New England communities "sold off" lawbreakers and unruly children in the hope of reforming them. A Connecticut law stated that boys should be bound out until the age of twenty-one and girls until eighteen or the time of their marriage if their parents allowed them "to live idly or misspend their time in loitering."

"Loitering" or idleness was a sin to the Puritans. In their eyes it was the single greatest threat to morality and social stability the community faced. Therefore, providing children, especially poor children, with the weapon of work with which to fight idleness was an act of charity. Work was good for children. And children's work was good for the community. Thus, the Puritans were concerned that their children received not only book learning, but also training in "labor and other employments which may be profitable to the Commonwealth."

These two themes of child labor, philanthropy and practicality, were in evidence throughout the colonial period. From Jamestown to Boston, spinning schools were suggested or erected "for the education of the poor" and the development of the clothmaking industry. As early as 1640 the magistrates of Massachusetts Bay were directed to investigate "what course may be taken for teaching the boys and girles in all towns the spinning of the yarne." At about the same time the people of Rowley, Massachusetts, were praised because they had "built a fulling mill, and caused their little ones to be very diligent in spinning cotten wool." And a hundred years later the same kind of thinking led to the formation of The Society for Encouraging Industry and Employing the Poor. It set out to promote the manufacture of woolen and other cloth and to employ "our own women and children who are now in a great measure idle."

Over time the colonists stopped speaking of the virtue of industry and stressed its practical value alone, especially where children were concerned. Virginians had always emphasized the commercial side of child labor and eventually even New Englanders came to adopt this point of view. By the second half of the eighteenth century, when vigorous efforts were being made to develop domestic manufactures, children were often spoken of as a national asset. Their labor was going to help make America great. And on the eve of the Revolution the colonists were busy congratulating themselves because children were in on every step of the new industrial development. As the governor of New York reported with delight, "Every house swarms with children, who are set to work as soon as they are able to spin and card." Given this heritage, it seemed quite natural for Americans to depend upon child labor when the Industrial Revolution crossed the Atlantic in the nineteenth century.

CHAPTER SEVEN
OUT OF MANY, ONE

In colonial times American society was remarkably homogeneous. Ninety-seven percent of the population lived in rural communities, few people were either very rich or very poor, and, except for the blacks, almost everyone blended easily with the white Anglo-Saxon majority. Then in the nineteenth century all that changed. American society—and its childhood experiences—developed great contrasts between immigrant and native-born, city dweller and country dweller, rich and poor. Much of this diversity was caused by industrialization. Starting with a handful of minor manufacturers at the time of the Revolution, America went on to become the mightiest industrial nation on earth by 1900. During the period of development, many youngsters took a turn at the machines as they had in colonial times.

"A LITTLE HARD WORK NEVER HURT ANYBODY"

In the early years of the Republic, children could be found wherever goods were manufactured. They worked in textile mills, shoe factories, and glassworks as well as their more traditional places, the farm and the craft shop. Even in the Utopian communities of the era, such as Brook Farm and New Harmony, children over ten were expected to do a full share of the work.

Of all the children employed in those early nineteenth-century factories, the girls who were hired to work in the textile mills of Lowell, Massachusetts, were considered the luckiest. They were far better fed, clothed, and educated than the ordinary factory hand and the treatment accorded them was said to resemble that of a sedate boarding school. But even Lowell was far from being a paradise for children. They had to put in very long hours at work, do their household chores, and attend evening school besides. In *An Idyl of Work* Lucy Larcom points out the drawbacks to working at Lowell:

> We must learn
> While we are children, how to do hard things,
> And that will toughen us, so Mother says;
> And she has worked hard always. When I first
> Learned to doff bobbins, I just thought it play.
> But when you do the same thing twenty times—
> A hundred times a day, it is so dull.

Dullness was often the least of the little workers' problems. As the nineteenth century wore on many of them were trapped in airless, rat-infested meat-packing plants or pitch-black coal mines for ten to fourteen hours at a stretch. Others had to tend dangerous machines whose whirring blades could gobble up a hand or even a whole arm before a child knew what had hit him. And, while American children were not subjected to the kind of gross brutality commonly inflicted upon little British workers, corporal punishment was not unknown. The mere dollar or two these children received hardly seemed worth the effort, but poor, greedy, or indifferent parents were often all too willing to sacrifice their offspring to get it.

Americans felt some sympathy for the plight of factory children, but they never doubted the correctness of child labor as such. The old Puritan belief in work was too deeply entrenched for that. True, factory hours were long and conditions in them harsh, but, they reasoned, how better could a poor child prepare for the life of drudgery which lay ahead of him? Moreover,

newspapers, novels, and even schoolbooks of the time romanticized poverty and glorified working one's way up from the
bottom. Little boys were constantly being reminded that steel
magnate Andrew Carnegie had started out in the mid-nineteenth century tending cotton machines for $1.20 a week—and
just look how he ended up.

Thus conditioned to favor child labor, the public placidly
accepted the glowing portrait of it painted by industrialists.
According to the factory owners they were actually doing the
children—and the public—a service by taking poor youngsters
off the streets and keeping them out of trouble. The factory
owners were also careful to stress the financial benefits reaped
by the young laborers, each of whom was depicted as the sole
support of his widowed mother. Finally, they congratulated
themselves for starting so many children on the ladder to
success.

What the industrialists' publicity failed to mention was that
almost none of their young workers could read or write, having
no opportunity to attend school. Nor did they get a chance to
play like other children in wholesome fresh air. Instead of
climbing the ladder to success, most young workers found
themselves stuck on the treadmill of inescapable poverty.

A few people understood that incarceration in a factory was
not what the Puritans had in mind when they espoused their
famous work ethic. To correct the worst abuses of the system,
they called for compulsory education laws and minimum-age
and maximum-hour requirements for all young workers. Their
efforts bore some fruit. As early as 1813 Connecticut passed a
law requiring the education of children in "manufactures," and
other states passed even more comprehensive "wrongs to
children" laws. However, since no proof of age was required
for employment and no money was allocated for enforcement,
most of these laws proved as ineffectual as similar bills passed
over and over again in England. For decades it was business as
usual in America where child labor was concerned.

By the end of the century, however, the dimensions of the

problem grew too great to be shrugged off any longer. In 1880 the United States Census revealed that one million children between the ages of ten and fifteen were holding down jobs. By the next Census that figure had skyrocketed to 1,750,000. In some fields children were particularly conspicuous. By 1900 over 30 percent of the employees in Southern mills were young-sters and in 1902, when they struck the coal fields, 20 percent of the United Mine Workers of America were boys. In addition there were thousands of children who did much of the marginal work of the city. They gathered rags, shined shoes, hawked newspapers, and roamed the streets peddling everything from strawberries to suspenders.

During the Progressive Era—1900–1920—reformers attacked many of America's ills: corruption in government, unfair competition in business, unhealthful handling of food—and the abuses of child labor. Some of the reformers banded together in the National Child Labor Committee to lobby for legal protection for young workers. They celebrated a real breakthrough in 1908 with *Muller* v. *Oregon*. Although the Supreme Court actually addressed itself here to the question of regulating working conditions for women, the Court's decision had the effect of gaining improvements for children as well. After *Muller* the minimum age at which children could be employed started at ten and eventually rose to sixteen in many states. In addition many new precautions were mandated to insure the health and safety of young workers. After 1900 these laws and the ones requiring school attendance helped dramati-cally reduce the number of children at work. In 1938 the Wages and Hours Act abolished child labor altogether in interstate commerce.

CITY LIGHTS

The Industrial Revolution was paralleled by an equally startling Urban Revolution. All across America in the nineteenth cen-tury new cities were springing up and old ones were expanding, spawning additional bedroom communities and small industrial towns. Whereas only 3 percent of all Americans had lived in urban areas in 1775, almost 50 percent of them were city dwellers by 1910, and, in some industrialized parts of the country, the proportion went much higher.

With cities regularly doubling, tripling, even quadrupling in size, it is little wonder that services and facilities failed to keep up. The city's inhabitants had to endure dirty water, foul smells, and cramped quarters as a matter of course. All these, adults and children suffered to the same degree, but when it came to the cities' almost complete lack of open space, it was the children who suffered most. In the country they were never far from woods and meadows which provided endless natural playgrounds. But in the city they had only narrow, crowded sidewalks in which to amuse themselves.

So little thought had been given to children's recreational needs that several large cities devoted more of their land to cemeteries than to parks. The lack of open space was partially a consequence of the city's haphazard growth, but it was also a sign of America's longstanding indifference—if not hostility—to play. In the nineteenth century this aspect of Puritanism was still strong enough for the authors of a children's book of games to declare: "We would wish it to be understood that we are far, very far, from being willing to encourage more [play] of any kind."

Only slowly did there develop an appreciation of play and the benefits it could bring to children, especially poor city children. Following the lead of German educators, a women's charitable organization had heaps of sand dumped at two locations in Boston in 1885. The neighborhood children seemed to enjoy them, so the following year three heaps of sand were set out. Thus was born the American playground. Later, under the leadership of the Playground Association of America, Progressive "child savers" worked for municipally funded, expertly supervised recreation areas for children. They were spectacularly successful. By 1915 over 430 cities had carved out parks and playgrounds, and thousands more soon followed suit. Today the idea is so commonly accepted that no one would think of putting up a school or an apartment house complex without making provisions for play.

HEADING FOR TROUBLE

Why should I have children? . . . They say the children here is all ruined—I know it. . . . They makes *'em thieves."*

—An Irish mother, New York City, 1853

One reason reformers so eagerly embraced the playground movement is that all around them they saw poor city children heading for trouble. Official reports corroborated their observations: juvenile delinquency and promiscuity were on the rise in the late nineteenth century. The traditional sources of discipline—family, church, school, community ties—did not keep children in line in the city as they had in the country. Nor did children have farm chores to keep them busy or free space in which to burn up excess energy. It was hoped that supervised playgrounds, by filling both the disciplinary and recreational voids in city life, would make children "good."

Another reason reformers favored supervised play is that it was supposed to teach immigrant children "American" values, such as obedience to authority and loyalty to the team. These values in turn were supposed to keep the newcomers on the straight and narrow path in this country. Concern with immigrant children was uppermost in the minds of Progressive "child savers," because immigrants then constituted the bulk, if not the entirety, of the nation's slums. Their children had a lot to contend with. Of peasant origins, they had to adjust to city ways, to a new language, and to different customs which often brought them into conflict with their parents. Families were strained and often broken as the members struggled to make these adjustments and to make them under the worst conditions of poverty.

Given these circumstances, it is understandable to us that first- and second-generation immigrant children accounted for half the inmates in reformatories and houses of refuge. But most Americans of that time chose not to understand but rather to condemn. Long prejudiced against foreigners in general and now against the new immigrants from Italy, Poland, and Russia in particular, Americans blamed inherited traits for the immigrant children's misbehavior or failure to make good. As the respected children's magazine *The Youth's Companion* put it: "The [young criminals] are mostly children of foreigners who live in garrets and cellars, who are themselves thriftless and indolent. . . ."

Contempt for immigrants was part of the overall hostility Americans felt toward the poor. They might cheer on the young hero of a book as he battled his way up from rags to riches; but if such a child showed up in real life, a middle-class mother would shoo him away quickly before he could contaminate her children with his "bad blood." There had always been some poor people in America, but with industrialization and immigration there were now many more of them. Americans looked at the teeming slums and grew frightened. They were terrified that poor children might band together in mobs, destroying property, attacking citizens, and ultimately fomenting political chaos.

To prevent such occurrences and to save these children from a life of crime, private charities and city agencies began to act. More and more they assumed responsibility for the poor, rootless children in their midst. Over the course of the nineteenth century countless industrial homes, camps, reformatories, missions, farm schools, newsboys' shelters, and asylums of various kinds were built. Some of these places merely provided free beds, others taught children trades and academic subjects as well.

Many of these children had no other place to go home to, because they were orphans. In colonial times they would have been packed off to a relative or "sold" at a town auction. But, with the arrival of cheap Irish labor in the 1840s, bonded servitude, already on the wane, ended completely. Americans preferred to hire an adult immigrant servant rather than take on the responsibility of bringing up an orphan. As for relatives, poor slum dwellers hardly had the space or money for their own children, much less for a dead brother's daughter.

Orphanages took their place. On paper these institutions sounded like a fine idea, but in reality they were often cold, harsh places where children were treated more like prison inmates than cherished family members. In nineteenth-century novels the orphan cut a universally popular figure. His triumphs were applauded, his troubles sighed over, and whenever "Our Hero" escaped from the orphanage, he won as much sympathy as any runaway slave.

An imaginative alternative to the orphanage was the foster home scheme of the Children's Aid Society. Starting in 1854 the Society sent some twenty thousand homeless children out West, where farmers took them into their homes. For many of the children, about half of whom were immigrants or the offspring of immigrants, the arrangement worked out quite well. In time the "child savers" began to see that the intimate atmosphere of a home was preferable to the impersonal atmosphere of an institution. Today orphanages are all but extinct while foster home care is used extensively.

Underlying the Children's Aid Society program was the belief that the city was no place to raise a child. Americans associated the city with crime, corruption, adult vices, and unsanitary living conditions. Although they continued to flock there for the job opportunities and social advantages the city offered, they clung to the notion that the country was the only true America. Therefore, growing up in the country had to be the only true childhood. It is no accident that Mark Twain set his idyll of nineteenth-century youth, *Tom Sawyer,* in a sleepy little village close to the great outdoors. And Kate Douglas Wiggins, the author of *Rebecca of Sunnybrook Farm,* went so far as to declare that every child "has a right to a genuine, free, serene, healthy, bread-and-butter childhood"—on the farm, of course. Although most parents could not produce a farm, they could move to the suburbs. And many of them did just that in the twentieth century, for the sake of the children.

Some young people managed to live in the city and still enjoy a privileged childhood. These were the offspring of the rich. They lived in large houses, were cared for by European governesses, and were driven about in elegant coaches. Lest they be contaminated by mingling with the lower classes, these wealthy children were either tutored at home or sent to private schools with others of their social circle. They were always carefully supervised whether at dancing class, on a walk downtown, or in a neighborhood park, which was occasionally encircled with a locked fence to keep out the riffraff of the city. Some upper-class children enjoyed the same relaxed give-and-take with their parents as middle-class children, but others had to endure a stiff formality imported from Great Britain. Like their British counterparts, these children were segregated in third-floor nurseries and were only summoned before their parents for an hour a day. But no matter what their regimen, upper- and middle-class children generally lived highly regulated, uneventful lives in nineteenth-century America.

But that is not to say that they didn't have any fun. Without T.V., or maybe because of its lack, they seem to have been very resourceful in amusing themselves. They put on plays, made up games, and invented elaborate battles for their toy soldiers and exquisite tea parties for their dolls. Rich American children had always been able to choose from a great variety of toys, most of which were imported from Europe. When the toy industry developed here after the Civil War, middle-class and even lower-class children could make their selections from a wide range of man-made amusements, too. In addition to the perennial favorites, such as marbles, kites, blocks, and balls, American manufacturers produced all kinds of miniatures, electric trains, Wild West drums, and optical sets. They also catered to the Victorian child's love of anything that moved or that moved him. This is evident in the 1877 Montgomery Ward catalogue—the first to advertise toys—which announced the sale of a number of rocking horses, sleds, doll carriages, and four sizes of tricycles costing from $3.15 to $5.85.

During the nineteenth century the city encompassed two extremes in society, the rich and the poor. The Southern plantation encompassed two others, the free and the enslaved.

THE SOUTH

For the master's children, life on the plantation was but a dream. As Letitia M. Burwell wrote in *A Girl's Life in Virginia,* "no young princesses could have received from admiring subjects more adulation" than she and her sister received from the "servants," as they genteelly referred to their slaves. Although most Southern whites were poor, upper-class children like the Burwells did live like princes and princesses. They were pampered, petted, waited on hand and foot. One ex-slave recalled that the master's children had been "mos'ly carried roun on pillows till dey big 'nough to walk . . . wouldn't let'em sit up till dey one year old." One such privileged child recalled that upon reaching the age of five he was given a pony, a shotgun, and his own slave "play child" to both accompany and serve him.

As the rich white children got older, the idyll continued. Since manual labor was considered degrading in that section of the country, girls were not taught anything useful. Nor were they taught much in the way of academic subjects, either. Their total education usually consisted of the three R's, a smattering of French, dancing, and perhaps drawing pretty pictures. According to one Southerner, more education was "considered queer." A mystique grew up around Southern belles, who were supposed to be beautiful and charming, but dumb. Since they ran large, complicated households of their own once they got married, these girls must have learned by observation, and many of them must have been quite bright underneath their frivolous façades.

Little more was expected of Southern boys than of Southern belles. Since most of the wealthy ones were not preparing for any vocation but that of gentlemen, they viewed school as a pleasant interlude before returning to the plantation. The president of a Georgia college complained that most of his students spent more time dueling, hunting, drinking, and gambling than on their courses. And in the late 1830s a Harvard student described his Southern classmates as having "charming manners, social aptitudes, imperious ways, abundant leisure, and plenty of money."

How different was the lot of the slave children who lived just across the yard from these privileged boys and girls. In the slaves' quarters the children did not know their birthdays, their fathers, and sometimes even their mothers, who might have been sold off to another master without them. Even when slave families did live together, the grownups were too exhausted from their field work and household chores to pay much attention to their offspring. Emotionally, slave children were on their own.

Since slave mothers had to return to the fields within three weeks of giving birth, their babies were left with females too old or too young to work. On the small farms these arrangements were informal, but on the larger plantations organized nurseries did the job. From all accounts slave nurseries were sad places. Frederick Law Olmsted described one in *Journey in the Back Country:* "Very few of the babies were in arms. Such as were not, generally lay on the floor, rolling about or sat still sucking their thumbs." Olmsted thought that the Negro woman in charge looked very kindly but he noted that she ignored the children. Apparently used to this kind of indifference, not one baby cried. And Olmsted said he never heard cries in any of the other nurseries he visited, either.

Slave children were fed a boring diet that consisted mainly of "mush," a coarse, boiled corn mixture. This food was set out on the floor in a large wooden bowl. At feeding time all the children crowded around the bowl, desperately trying to scoop up enough mush with their fingers or a bit of shell to feel satisfied. They rarely succeeded. Slave children were often given just one garment to wear, a coarse shirt that came down to their knees. If this shirt wore out before the next clothing allowance day, they went naked—no matter what the season. Without coats, sweaters, or shoes, the children were often miserably cold. They went to sleep on the dirt floor of their cabins shivering under the old sack or one thin blanket that constituted the whole of their "bed."

From the age of six, children were gradually broken in to the routine of work. At first their chores were small: sweeping yards, running errands, carrying water to the men and women in the fields. By the age of ten they were holding down regular work assignments. A lucky few were brought into the big house as servants or taught a trade. For most, though, it was back-breaking field work from "can see to can't see." As the children grew up they experienced the overseer's lash, master's cane, and the thousand and one indignities that went with being a slave.

Despite Southern propaganda about the contented black man, every slave knew he was being deprived, even the youngest ones. Black children saw the good things that white children had and, like any human being, they wanted them, too. They longed for the ginger cakes, the birthday parties, and, above all, the education. But the last item especially was forbidden to them. As a young slave in Baltimore, Frederick Douglass was lucky enough to have a mistress who taught him the ABCs.

When her husband found out about it, he was furious. Douglass, who later ran away and became a great abolitionist, recorded the master's reaction in his autobiography:

> If you give a nigger an inch, he will take an ell. A nigger should know nothing but to obey his master—to do as he is told to do. Learning would *spoil* the best nigger in the world. Now, said he, if you teach that nigger (speaking of myself) how to read, there will be no keeping him. It would forever unfit him to be a slave. He would at once become unmanageable, and of no value to his master. As to himself, it could do him no good, but a great deal of harm. It would make him discontented and unhappy.

But Douglass persevered in his efforts. He got some young white apprentices to teach him to read. Although the white boys were not much better off than he at the time, Douglass envied them their future. "You will be free as soon as you are twenty-one," he told them, "*but I am a slave for life! Have I not as good a right to be free as you have?*" By abolishing slavery, the Thirteenth Amendment of the Constitution gave every black person that right.

EDUCATION

The determination of white Southerners to keep their slaves from getting an education is a testimonial to the American belief in its power. Education was supposed to be the key to everything: to successful democracy, to material growth, and to individual enrichment. Yet despite these widely held sentiments, most American children were getting little or no education in the early years of the Republic. Some children lived too far away from any school to attend, while others lived close enough but had to work while school was in session. Some parents didn't have the money to send their children to tuition academies; others had the money but didn't want to waste it on anything as frivolous—or potentially dangerous—as education. And when it came to supporting a system that would provide instruction to other people's children, especially the poor, Americans kept a tight grip on the purse strings.

The physical condition of schools reflected these attitudes. Frontier children often attended class in sod huts, Southern children still trekked to dilapidated, old field buildings, and city pupils crowded into dark, musty structures that were hazardous to both their health and their safety. At mid-century Boston's school system, considered a model for the nation, consisted of 161 one-room village schoolhouses which had simply been annexed as the city grew. Everywhere walls were barren of cheery illustrations, and the standardized desks, chairs, and benches took no account of the different-sized children who had to use them.

In these early days of public school education, guidelines were extremely flexible. There were no fixed sequences of study, no customary ages for attendance, no generally accepted criteria for advancement. Every county and every community handled education its own way. The quality of instruction these localities offered was generally low, because few of the teachers were college graduates and none had been professionally trained. In the 1850s an applicant who came before an Indiana school board was asked what preparation he had made for teaching school. "I have got my corn shucked, my winter's wood cut." The interviewer's reaction? "You will do."

Not everyone was so easily satisfied, however. Leaders of the common school movement sought to raise the level of instruction through teacher training institutes and the imposition of uniform standards on all school districts. They also wanted to see public school education made available to all, paid for by all, and backed up by compulsory attendance laws. Under the prodding of Horace Mann, Massachusetts led the way in 1827 with America's first free, tax-supported, state-wide school system.

Leaders of the common school movement did not stop there.

They went on to try to take secondary education out of the realm of private academies and into the network of the public schools. Few communities were willing to undertake this additional tax burden, however, and in 1860 there were only 320 or so high schools in America, over half of them in the three progressive states of Massachusetts, New York, and Ohio. At the end of the century a mere 11 percent of all high school age children were enrolled in the public schools. After that the demand for secondary education grew until today almost everyone between the ages of fourteen and seventeen is still a student.

After the Civil War every Southern state mandated free public education, but the region was too poor to provide much of it. As they had in colonial times, Southern children lagged behind Northerners in schooling. Black Southern children lagged farthest behind of all, because their schools received only half as much money as white schools in the region. Reporting on the situation in Atlanta, Georgia, in 1906, one journalist observed: "The Negro is neglected. Several new schools have been built for white children, but there has been no school for colored children in 15 or 20 years. . . ." Along with other factors, this lack of a good education prevented black children from fulfilling the promise of freedom.

" . . . TAUGHT TO THE TUNE OF A HICKORY STICK"

Dear Teacher:
   . . . When we go into the world, we shall not forget to whom we owe our acquirements, but shall remember you ever with almost filial regard. Whenever memory recalls our school days, our hearts will warm toward you as they do to-day.

*   *   *

No more school, no more books,
No more cross-eyed teacher's looks.
                    —Year's end, late nineteenth century

In the first half of the nineteenth century the public school master was often a ne'er-do-well like his colonial predecessor. He gave out assignments, listened to recitations, and sometimes swept the floor and washed the windows as well. A large part of his time seems to have been devoted to keeping order, a task he accomplished with frequent canings. With the full approval of parents, the nineteenth-century master acted on the principle that corporal punishment was necessary to train children and savages, two groups he often mentioned in the same breath. While his methods often seemed harsh, there is evidence that it was not all give and no take. In *The Hoosier School Master,* a local trustee is reported to have warned a rather delicate-looking young aspirant:

> Want to become a school-master, do you? You? Well, what would *you* do in the Flat Creek Deestrick, *I'd* like to know? Why, the boys have driv off the last two, and licked the one afore them like blazes. . . . They'd pitch you out of doors, sonny, neck and heels, afore Christmas.

With more and more children going to school, school boards began to cast about for additional teachers. Throughout our history women had been hired to fill in while the male teachers were out harvesting crops or were otherwise unavailable, but now women were sought after for permanent positions. Women offered several advantages over the male schoolmasters. They were generally better educated, in greater supply, and more willing to make teaching their life's work despite the poor pay and low prestige. In time the typical American teacher was a woman, not a man.

The first two visible results of this changeover were an improvement in the quality of instruction and an abandonment of corporal punishment as a daily occurrence. Some children were still beaten, but only for the most serious offenses. Even then it was a male principal who usually administered the caning, because it was not considered seemly for a woman to beat children.

But chaos did not ensue. If anything the atmosphere in the classroom grew more controlled as the century wore on. There never seemed to be a relaxed moment, never a break when the children were permitted to chatter among themselves. Instead they were kept hard at work memorizing grammar rules, doing arithmetic drills, and giving oral recitations while standing at attention. Teachers maintained their absolute control by teaching everyone the same thing at the same time. They also had the pupils repeat their lessons aloud in unison. Indeed, repetition was considered the key to learning, "repetition until the things you learned beat in your brain even at night when you were falling asleep," as one former student described it. Some teachers went to extreme lengths to obtain tidiness in education. One woman lined up her students along the edge of a floorboard for a recitation. Dissatisfied with the effect, she exclaimed, "How can you learn anything with your knees and toes out of order?"

Teachers had fewer educational tools than they have today, but one of their standards was Noah Webster's *"Blue-Backed Speller."* Spelling was very important in those days and Webster's formed the basis of the spelling bees which were often the highlight of the school—and community—calendar. Arithmetic books had many of the same problems in them as today's texts, but nineteenth-century children worked them out on slates instead of paper. The children were supposed to wipe off their slates with a damp cloth. However, little boys found it more convenient to use a little spit and a shirtsleeve and, for the fast erasure of a caricature, even a moistened thumb would do.

The most important teaching aids of all were the McGuffey *Eclectic Readers.* They sold some 130 million copies in various levels and editions, becoming to the nineteenth century what *The New England Primer* had been to the eighteenth: the reflector and creator of basic American attitudes. The sixth McGuffey *Reader* might have included excerpts from Shakespeare, the Bible, Dickens, and Henry Wadsworth Longfellow, while the simpler first *Reader* might have featured "Twinkle, Twinkle, Little Star" and "Mary Had a Little Lamb." But few of the selections at any level were chosen just for their entertainment value. In addition to serving as examples of good literary style, they were supposed to point a moral. In story after story perseverance, generosity, kindness, thrift, patriotism, hard work, and the other fundamental virtues were extolled. The second reader's version of George Washington and the cherry tree is typical of the way McGuffey got his message across:

> "George," said his father, "do you know who killed that fine cherry-tree yonder in the garden?" This was a hard question; George was silent for a moment; and then, looking at his father, his young face bright with conscious love of truth, he bravely cried out: "I can't tell a lie, father; you know, I can't tell a lie. I did cut it with my hatchet."
>
> "Come to my arms, my dearest boy!" cried his father, in transports: "come to my arms! you killed my cherry-tree, George, but you have now paid me for it a thousandfold. Such proof of heroic truth in my son is of more value than a thousand trees, though they were all of the purest gold."

THE GUARANTEE

Education was free. That subject my father had written about repeatedly, as comprising his chief hope for us children, the essence of American opportunity, the treasure that no thief could touch, not even misfortune or poverty. It was the one thing that he was able to promise us when he sent for us: surer, safer than bread or shelter. On our second day I was thrilled with the realization of what this freedom of education meant. A little girl from across the alley came and offered to conduct us to school. My father was out, but we five

between us had a few words of English by this time. We
knew the word school. We understood. This child, who
had never seen us till yesterday, who could not pro-
nounce our names, who was not much better dressed
than we, was able to offer us the freedom of the schools
of Boston! No applications made, no questions asked,
no examinations, rulings, exclusions; no machinations,
no fees. The doors stood open for every one of us. The
smallest child could show us the way.
                              —Mary Antin, *The Promised Land*

Mary Antin, a Jewish immigrant who had been denied schooling in Russia because of her religion, appreciated the unique
character of American education: the fact that it was open to
all. In other countries a child was expected to be what his
parent was—peasant, mechanic, tradesman, or professional—
and he was educated accordingly. But in America everyone
was expected to rise as high as his abilities could take him
regardless of what his father did. From the start this democratic
ideal was built into the public school system. Education was to
be made available to all the children—smart and dull, good and
bad, white and, eventually, black. No one was to be cut early
or channeled into a vocational program at a young age as was
the practice in Europe. The true importance of the American
public school system, then, was not that it taught democracy
but that it *created* it. And as society demanded greater literacy
and more technical skills, the public school's contribution to
equality of opportunity became even more important. Indeed,
the inclusion of poor children at the high school level was
considered one of the major egalitarian advances of the nineteenth century.

In addition to enhancing the promise of democracy, the
public school system was remarkably successful in fulfilling the
other goals set for it. It created one people out of many
peoples. It did this with the aid of mass-produced textbooks,
which gave all American children a common cultural background. Secondly, it spread a certain lasting set of values

across the land. Forty years after they finished their last *Reader,* for example, people reported that McGuffey had so imbued them with the idea of thrift that it was physically impossible for them to throw away anything which might some-day be useful. Thirdly, the public school system allowed new-comers to enter American society on an equal footing with natives. It taught them English, history, and patriotic exercises such as the salute to the flag. Humorist Harry Golden, who lived through the experience himself, describes the Americani-zation of an immigrant child:

> When a new greenhorn came to the class, frightened and con-fused, unable to manage any English, all knew that within six months he would be able to stand before us and, heavy accent and all, recite:
>
> > I love the name of Washington,
> > I love my country, too.
> > I love the flag, the dear old flag,
> > The red, the white, the blue.

Finally, the public school system offered American children something priceless—an absolute sense of security. According to Harry Golden: "On the Lower East Side in the early years of this century we came as close to any guarantee as life has ever offered. The guarantee was if you worked hard, went to school, studied and saved, you could participate in America." And the great lawyer Clarence Darrow, in recalling all the moral teach-ings of his Ohio school days, remembered feeling that "if we did these things, some fairy godmother would come along and give us everything our hearts desired." How many of today's children can look to the future with such assurance?

MOVING CENTER STAGE

It was a misfortune to have been born when children were nothing and to live until men were nothing.
—Ralph Waldo Emerson, quoting a "witty friend"

The attention lavished on the public school system is indicative of the increasing importance of children as the nineteenth century wore on. The development of pediatric medicine, the campaign for clean milk, the playground movement and the "child study" movement all reflect a growing concern for their welfare. Indeed, to judge from the torrent of advice on the subject, what to *do* about children was becoming a national obsession.

Even as childhood was being accorded higher status it was changing. It was losing its variety, because, thanks to compulsory attendance laws, almost everyone was going to school. It was also stretching out because education was taking longer. Whereas some colonial children were earning a living by the age of ten or twelve, most late nineteenth-century children were not financially independent until the age of sixteen, eighteen, or even older. The institution of the school was also at the heart of childhood's increasing alienation from adulthood. Removed from the daily activities of society, schoolchildren were now considered a breed apart. Their world was identified by the special clothing, toys, sports equipment, and literature that developed at the same time and for the same reason in Europe.

Girlhood changed even more radically than boyhood. Traditionally, American females were brought up to be high-principled and gentle—but humorless, artificial, uninformed, and unambitious. Since the goal set for them was catching a husband, all their early training was directed toward making them pleasing to men. And since men were supposed to be pleased by girls who were beautiful but dumb, this meant they received little formal education. Men were also supposed to be attracted to frail women whom they could protect. Since the ideal Victorian girl had delicate nerves and little physical stamina, "Our Heroine" was always fainting away.

As early as the Civil War, some American girls started to shed their false fragility. Although it would take a long time for the others to catch up, this small number began to swim, skate, play tennis, and, when bicycling became popular, go riding along with the boys. Nor did they become old maids as a result. In 1862 the *Atlantic Monthly* reported that "health is coming into fashion" and in some localities "if a girl could vault a five-barred gate, her prospects for a husband were considered to be improved ten per cent."

After the Civil War it also became socially acceptable for girls to acquire a decent education. Many of the women most sought after by men were now graduates of high schools, state universities, and the new prestigious women's colleges—Vassar, Wellesley, Mills, and Smith. But girls did not have to settle for marriage alone. For the first time they could aspire to respectable careers as teachers or office workers, options a number of them chose to exercise.

For those who did get married there were new challenges in family life as well. Although fathers were still the head of the household, they were increasingly absent, leaving mothers to take over primary responsibility for bringing up the children. Then, too, nineteenth-century mothers generally had fewer offspring than their colonial counterparts, but they paid more attention to each one.

Although many women strove valiantly, they were not able to stem the erosion of family life caused by urbanization and industrialization. Over the course of the nineteenth century the family was stripped of many of its traditional roles. The school took over its moral and educational functions and other institutions took over much of the rest. This phenomenon was to have far-reaching consequences for childhood in the twentieth century. As educator Ellwood Patterson Cubberly so accurately predicted: "Each year the child is coming to belong more and more to the state, and less and less to the parent."

CHAPTER EIGHT

THE CENTURY OF
THE CHILD

In the early years of the 1900s reformers confidently predicted that this would be "the century of the child." At long last the child was to be rescued from the ignorance, neglect, and outright abuse which had so often characterized his treatment in the past. New research tools harnessed to right thinking were going to illuminate the "one best way" to raise and educate children. The early signs were encouraging: in 1909 President Theodore Roosevelt convened the first White House Conference on Children; in 1912 the U.S. Children's Bureau was established; in 1918 a Child Health Day was declared, followed by Baby Week and, in 1919, Children's Year. Much of the heightened interest in childhood stemmed from a new absorption in the biological and social sciences, especially psychology. Suddenly children acquired new status as subjects of legitimate scientific inquiry. People began to feel that an understanding of child behavior could unlock the secret of adult behavior and shed light on the mysterious historical development of the human species.

PSYCHOLOGY: "THE CHILD IS FATHER OF THE MAN"

The nature of childhood had long been the object of contemplative thought. But, starting with Charles Darwin's *Origin of Species* in 1859, it became the subject of scientific analysis as well. Suddenly, people began to see in the child's behavior a

All city facilities had trouble keeping up with their soaring populations, but schools were the most burdened down. Here, a jam-packed New York City classroom at the turn of the century. (Museum of the City of New York.)

There was more watching than playing at this early playground as students waited to take their turn on the equipment. (Museum of the City of New York.)

This young employee of a Virginia glass factory sometimes worked all night. (Museum of the City of New York.)

Although obviously idealized, this portrait of four sisters made some attempt to show them as they really were. The acceptance of children as children is essentially a twentieth-century phenomenon. (Museum of the City of New York.)

The poor, orphaned street boy tugged at the heartstrings of moviegoers through countless reels. One of the most popular of these unfortunates was Jackie Coogan, shown here in The Kid. (The Museum of Modern Art/Film Stills Archives.)

Adolescence was supposed to be carefree in America— at least that's how it was portrayed before World War II. Here, perennial teenagers June Preisser, Mickey Rooney, and Judy Garland are shown emerging from that teenage heaven, the soda shop. (The Museum of Modern Art/Film Stills Archives.)

In the 1960's the civil rights movement focused on desegregating educational facilities. Sometimes this required federal intervention. (Wide World Photos.)

Dating we think from biblical times, hopscotch is one of those games that will be played as long as there are kids. (Jon W. Greenleaf.)

As long as we love to laugh, cry, dream, hope—to live—we will keep having children. (Jon W. Greenleaf.)

reenactment of man in his animal origins, man in his primitive state, and man in his early history, and they concocted elaborate theories based on these parallels. At the height of the movement a book appeared called *The Child: A Study of the Evolution of Man.*

Scientists also began to explore the nature of human development. Is the newborn child a blank slate, a *tabula rasa,* on which experience will carve the only lines, or is he already a totally formed human being with thoughts, emotions, and specific capabilities of his own? Nobody knew. Scientists sensed that the truth must fall somewhere in between, but they argued about which was more important in shaping an individual, his inherited traits or his early experiences and training. This debate, often referred to as "nature versus nurture," continues to rage today.

When the subject was first broached in the mid-nineteenth century, one of those who came out strongly for "nature" was Francis Galton. Galton made extensive use of the new mathematical tool of statistics to support his argument. Pointing to the repeated appearance of talent in some of the families he surveyed, Galton declared: "I have no patience with the hypothesis . . . that babies are born pretty much alike, and that the sole agencies in creating differences between boy and boy, and man and man, are steady application and moral effort."

This point of view was roundly disputed by the behaviorist John B. Watson. After writing his dissertation on the education of rats, Watson turned his attention to children, who, he felt, could be trained exactly the same way. To Watson variations in the "raw material" among infants was unimportant. "Nurture" or specific environmental experience was everything in shaping the individual. Watson led parents to believe that they could create exactly the kind of child they wanted by training him properly.

Both academic child psychology and practical child rearing would reel under the impact of Watson's theory for many years to come. But some scientists refused to take either his side or Galton's. Echoing the sentiments of many, child-development authority Arnold Gessell said that the distinction between nature and nurture was artificial, because they were interrelated phenomena and each had an important role to perform.

Thanks largely to the efforts of G. Stanley Hall, the "nature versus nurture" argument and other developments in the field of child study were brought to the attention of the scientific community and interested members of the public in the early twentieth century. Hall is considered the founder of child psychology in the United States. He started a journal to provide a forum for speculation and concrete findings on child behavior. He developed sophisticated questionnaires about children, and he supervised a busy corps of students who were charged with sending them out and evaluating them. He practically invented a stage of life with his two-volume work, *Adolescence*. And last, but certainly not least, he invited the Viennese psychiatrist Sigmund Freud to speak in the United States.

With his theory of infantile sexuality, Sigmund Freud singlehandedly remade the concept of childhood in the Western world. Until Freud . . .

> Childhood was looked upon as "innocent" and free from the lusts of sex, and the fight with the demon of "sensuality" was not thought to begin until the troubled age of puberty. Such occasional sexual activities as it had been impossible to overlook in children were put down as signs of degeneracy and premature depravity or as a curious freak of nature.
>
> —Sigmund Freud, *An Autobiographical Study*

In the late Victorian era, when Freud was developing his theories, the myth of childhood "innocence" was at its height. It satisfied both the religious and the psychological needs of a people terrified of sex. But Freud found in analyzing his patients that the myth simply was not true. He discovered that the child does have strong sexual drives, indeed that he is born with them, and that they will undergo several changes before reaching their adult form. The child's first sex objects are his own parents, a phenomenon known as the Oedipus complex.

Although Freud described the child as a sexual creature, the psychiatrist considered him in no way corrupted. He insisted that an infant could have no idea of right and wrong and, therefore, should not be judged by conventional moral standards. "The little child is above all shameless," he wrote, "and during its early years it sometimes evinces pleasure in displaying its body and especially its sexual organs." Freud warned against inhibiting these early natural impulses with too early or too strict training. Later psychological problems might be avoided, he wrote, "if the child's sexual life were allowed free play, as happens among many primitive races."

Statements such as this shocked the public, which reacted by mounting a vicious campaign against Freud. He was accused of having a dirty mind, of "soiling" childhood, and of undermining religion, morality, the family, and the very foundations of civilization. In America as much as in Europe, people found it hard to surrender their cherished myth of childhood's purity. Although the *Essay on Infant Sexuality* was published in 1905, it wasn't until at least two decades had passed that Freud's theories were widely accepted on this side of the Atlantic. Today, Freud's many contributions to our understanding of human behavior are taken for granted. Indeed, no one could espouse the *non*sexual nature of childhood without appearing ignorant, although many would disagree with Freud's definition of "sexual."

But Sigmund Freud did more for childhood than reveal its sexual component. He firmly established it as *the* critical period of life in terms of psychological development. It was only natural, then, that as psychology came to play more and more of a role in modern life, childhood would assume greater and greater importance along with it. Over the centuries the child had moved from the obscurity of the wings to a prominent place on the stage of human life. He had been promoted from bit player to supporting actor to featured performer. But it was only in the twentieth century, with the help of Sigmund Freud, that he became a star.

SCHOOLS: THE CHILD-CENTERED APPROACH

Even before Freudian ideas were widely accepted, psychological investigators had started to turn their attention toward the field of education. Several men tried to devise a "mental test" which would measure ability to learn or intelligence quotient (I.Q.). The Frenchman Albert Binet was the first one to do it successfully. His method, known in its translated, revised form as the Stanford-Binet Test, was adopted with almost reckless speed by American educators. For those seeking orderliness in education, the I.Q. test seemed to be a godsend. Here was a scientific method for knowing exactly how to categorize a student and therefore how to teach him. Even when the use of I.Q. tests on soldiers during World War I raised serious questions about what was really being measured—achievement (what had been learned) or aptitude (what could be learned)—educators refused to give them up. In fact, as the twentieth century progressed, psychological testing became more and more popular.

Educators justified the use of I.Q. testing on the grounds that it would enable them to tailor the education to suit the child. But, in reality, schools were becoming ever more rigid. Every child was expected to enter at the same early age and move up with his peers from grade to grade and classroom to classroom in neat, orderly fashion. Report cards labeled his progress and replaced the human contact the school had had with his home.

In the large district schools that replaced the old one-room schoolhouses, children sat for long hours on hard wooden seats chanting multiplication tables, memorizing dates, practicing penmanship, and copying out each corrected mistake twenty times. Chorus work, which was the only means of instruction, discouraged children from thinking for themselves. But this was not wholly accidental, for the passive, unquestioning student was the good student as far as educators were concerned. They looked upon the school as an assembly line and the children in it as so many interchangeable parts. As Ellwood Patterson Cubberly put it: "Our schools are, in a sense, factories in which the raw products (children) are to be shaped into products to meet the various demands of life."

Not everyone agreed with Cubberly. John Dewey, for one, developed a theory of progressive education in which school was a satisfying experience in itself as well as a processing plant for future citizens. For Dewey the child, not the curriculum, was at the heart of education. Incorporating Freudian ideas, Dewey sought to develop a curious and independent child, instead of the passive youngster the public schools insisted on. His first tenet was learning by doing.

As the years went by, some of John Dewey's followers and imitators began to carry his child-centered approach to extremes. They threw out all discipline, all book learning—and all common sense—in the interests of allowing the child to "express himself." Critics often used these excesses to discredit the whole progressive education movement. They felt that the school, like every other institution in America, should be adult-centered. Criticism of progressive education frequently took the form of ridicule, and by the 1930s the mere mention of it was sure to provoke laughter.

Despite the ridicule, progressive education contributed to a fundamental change in the American public school. It helped humanize or, rather, "childrenize" the atmosphere there. Over the course of the twentieth century desks and chairs were scaled down; artwork was pinned up; fish tanks were placed in halls; slick color pictures were added to texts; and films and records were incorporated into classroom studies. A new emphasis was placed on "enrichment" through special music and art classes and trips to museums. In addition, the child's feelings were considered as never before. To spare him from the pressures of competition, among other things, grades were done away with and teacher evaluations introduced in their stead. Being left back was also eliminated because it was considered psychologically damaging. The slow learner was now given an automatic promotion with extra help, theoretically, in the next grade.

Although the atmosphere in the classroom relaxed considerably, its fundamental mode of operations remained essentially the same. Then in the late 1960s, the open classroom was imported from Europe. The ultimate in child-centered schooling, the open classroom owed its existence to the spirit of John Dewey, the trials and errors of European teachers, and the theories of Swiss psychologist Jean Piaget.

Piaget said that children reason so differently from adults that they cannot be effectively taught the same way, i.e., from a book. Instead, children should have appropriate materials placed around the room which will enable them to "discover" knowledge. Gone were the neat rows of desks, the reading groups, the daily assignments and—especially—the silence. Now in many classrooms there were "activity centers," individual conferences, weekly contracts—and an unholy din. As the child moved along at his own pace, the rate of learning and much of the responsibility for it shifted from teacher to student.

Whether it was the fault of child-centered schooling, an overemphasis on enrichment, too much T.V., or other factors in American society, children did not seem to be learning their basic skills. Books such as *Why Johnny Can't Read* were an embarrassing indictment of the public school system. Yet it was not for lack of money that children were not learning, because at the same time that test scores were falling, taxpayers were spending more dollars on education than ever before. A new hue and cry arose that schools should "prove" they were doing their job and doing it efficiently. Since everyone's criteria for this differed so widely, test scores were once again emphasized as the ultimate standard of educational effectiveness. Frills started to lose favor and the old-fashioned drill was brought back.

The trend toward conservatism in education was given a large shove by the economic recession of the 1970s. School budgets were being slashed in September 1976 when *U.S. News & World Report* ran an article declaring, "Three R's in School Now: Retrenchment, Results, Realism." Does this mean the end of child-centered education in America? No. America will never return to the conditions of 1900. Experimentation has temporarily ceased on a mass scale, but with economic recovery and some new discovery about how children learn, it undoubtedly will be resumed.

LAW: CHILDREN'S RIGHTS

Even more controversial than the open classroom has been the interjection of civil rights into the field of education. Since 1954 when the Supreme Court ruled that "separate educational facilities are inherently unequal," the courts have actively been pursuing the goal of racial balance in the schools. They've ended legal segregation and attempted to do away with de facto segregation, although the latter aim has proved difficult to achieve. They've also stopped the practice of "tracking" or ability grouping, because it has had the effect of keeping the races apart even when they attend the same school.

The courts have begun to look into other school policies, too, that might infringe upon students' civil rights. In the 1975 case *Goss* v. *Lopez,* for example, the Supreme Court laid down a list of procedures that have to be followed when students are suspended. Declaring that "young people do not shed their rights at the schoolhouse door," the Court ruled that public school pupils cannot be suspended without notice of the charges against them, an explanation of any damaging evidence, and a chance to tell their side of the story.

Suspending students for misbehavior is of particular concern to civil rights advocates, because it seems to be used increasingly to keep minority children out of school. Today, more than 10 percent of the students in our cities (where most minorities live) are suspended once a year.

Many retarded or handicapped children are also out of school, but in their case it is because local schools are not equipped to handle them. Civil rights advocates claim that it is unconstitutional to deny these youngsters access to education and some courts have agreed, stating that a lack of specialized facilities is not a valid excuse for rejecting a student. In *Mills* v. *Board of Education,* for example, a district court ordered every excluded child to be readmitted to the Washington, D. C., schools "regardless of the degree of the child's mental, physical or emotional disability or impairment."

Yet nearly two million children are out of school today. According to the Children's Defense Fund, these students are not lightheartedly playing hooky. Many of them are migrant farm workers who move so frequently and work such long hours that they cannot attend school. Others live in remote areas, don't have transportation, can't afford proper clothes, or don't speak English. Still others have been excluded for pregnancy, alien status, and "ineducability." Some are behind bars.

But while most involved citizens feel that every one of these children has a right to education—and that society should translate that right into reality—a few people, advocates of a kind of "children's lib," feel that there should be a right *not* to go to school. Today, every state except Mississippi has compulsory education laws. These laws were considered a great step forward when they were enacted, because they enabled children to stop working and start studying. Ironically, compulsory education laws are being criticized now for the very reason that they prevent children from working and they don't give the youngsters any choice in the matter. Educator John Holt is one of the most articulate spokesmen for this point of view. In his book *Escape From Childhood,* Holt states:

> The requirement that a child go to school, for about six hours a day, 180 days a year, for about ten years, whether or not he learns anything there, whether or not he already knows it or could learn it faster or better somewhere else, is such a gross violation of civil liberties that few adults would stand for it. But the child who resists is treated as a criminal.

"PERSONS" UNDER THE CONSTITUTION

The concept of children's rights is growing and not just in the field of education. In 1957 the United Nations ratified the Declaration of the Rights of the Child. Thirteen years later the White House Conference on Children put youngsters' developmental, health, and educational needs in the same class as life, liberty, and the pursuit of happiness. It endorsed a children's Bill of Rights stating:

> We conceive of "rights" as the intrinsic entitlements of every human born or residing in the United States. . . . We must recognize children's inherent rights which, although not exclusively those established by law and enforced by the courts, are nonetheless closely related to the law.

And the law has been increasingly concerned with safeguarding the civil liberties of children. In the 1967 case *In re Gault,* the Supreme Court held that children in juvenile court were constitutionally entitled to certain due process guarantees: notice to parents and child of the charges and adequate time to prepare a defense; the right to counsel; privilege against self-incrimination; and right to cross-examine witnesses. The Court asserted that "neither the Fourteenth Amendment nor the Bill of Rights is for adults alone." Two years later in *Tinker* v. *Des Moines School District,* the Supreme Court opened the door to even wider rights for children by declaring them "persons" under the Constitution.

The *Gault* and *Tinker* decisions are remarkable, one might even say revolutionary, when considered in historical perspective. Down through the ages the child had no standing at all in the eyes of the law. He was considered a mere possession, albeit a prized possession, of the father who spoke and acted for him. A child was not allowed to exercise his own will, because he was incapable of deferring pleasure and making sensible decisions concerning his future—or so the argument ran. Better to let father make all the decisions; father knows best.

By and large the law still reflects this attitude. It can be seen in *Wisconsin* v. *Yoder,* the 1972 case in which the Supreme Court upheld the right of Amish parents not to send their children to high school as required by law, because it conflicted with their religious beliefs. Justice William O. Douglas concurred with the majority opinion for the one child who had spoken up in her own behalf. But he disagreed where the other children who had not testified were concerned. In his groundbreaking dissent he argued:

> While the parents, absent dissent, normally speak for the entire family, the education of the child is a matter on which the child will often have decided views. . . . It is the future of the student, not the future of the parents, that is imperilled in today's decision. . . . It is the student's judgment, not his parent's, that is essential if we are to give full meaning to what we have said about the Bill of Rights and the right of students to be masters of their own destiny.

Children's advocates heartily concur with Justice Douglas's line of reasoning because, they contend, a child's interests are not always identical to those of his parents. They want the law to treat the youngster as an independent entity. Moreover, they would like to see his minority or infancy status abolished and the presumption of his incompetency reversed. John Holt, for one, would give a child of any age the right to vote, hold a job, choose his own guardians, and set up his own household! But most people realize that even if children were granted these and every other adult right, many of them would still not be able to function autonomously in our society. Children need help. So, while some civil libertarians are fighting for more adult rights for children, other advocates are trying to get the youngsters' unique needs recognized and converted into legally enforceable rights.

Hindering both efforts is the frightening specter of juvenile crime. In America today youngsters under the age of twenty-one account for over 40 percent of all arrests and the percentage is growing rapidly. Their vandalism costs taxpayers well over a billion dollars a year, their street gangs are turning urban life into a nightmare. It is little wonder, then, that people are becoming more concerned about protection *from* children than for them. The fact that younger and younger children are committing more and more serious crimes underscores their fears. As a police officer said of this alarming trend: "Kids have changed, and the laws have not kept abreast of the times. . . . We've found that 13- and 14-year-olds are more likely to kill than adults; they don't grasp the consequences of their acts."

While some people feel that the system is too soft on juvenile offenders, some claim it is too harsh, especially for minor offenses. Children can now be arrested for acts which are criminal for adults and also for acts which are *not* criminal for adults. Among the latter are the status offenses, a grab bag of vague or innocuous activities such as smoking cigarettes, swearing, loitering, and waywardness. Few normal children have not used vulgar language or been "wayward" at one time or another. In fact, if Tom Sawyer were around today, he would probably be labeled a juvenile delinquent and clapped into jail.

Juvenile offenders are confined both for their own good and for that of society. But the facilities provided for them are so woefully inadequate that neither goal is realized. In all of New York, for example, there are only nine hundred places in the state-run training schools, and the length of stay is limited by law to eighteen months—even if a child has committed rape or murder. As it turns out, there is so much pressure to take in new offenders that most inmates are released after only nine months. Nor is this time well spent. The youngsters get little psychiatric help or vocational guidance from the correctional staff, while they get a great deal of help from their fellow inmates—in criminal techniques. Some of the children fare worse than others. According to retired family court judge Justine Wise Polier: "Unequal and inferior services, and the denial of services to children from minority groups, have shadowed every aspect of child care and juvenile justice."

Clearly, the system is in desperate need of reform. More juvenile courts have to be established beyond the few that now exist in our largest cities. Court procedures have to be brought into line with new trends in civil rights. Once sentenced, juvenile offenders should be separated according to their age and the seriousness of their crimes. Today, a child who is merely having trouble growing up too often finds himself incarcerated with highly disturbed youngsters or hardened adult criminals. Some juvenile proceedings should be decriminalized entirely. For example, Massachusetts recently dropped its designation "stubborn child" and substituted for it "child in need of services" (CHINS). At the same time the state made a real commitment to the rehabilitation (or habilitation) of youngsters in this category. Such a reorientation in thinking is necessary for every aspect of the juvenile justice system. Only when it occurs will we be able to fulfill the broad promise of children's rights.

ADOLESCENCE: SOMETHING NEW UNDER THE SUN

Teenagers have a bad reputation in America and crime is only one of the many factors contributing to it. Rock music, blue jeans, long hair, and "wild ways" are also held against them. Yet in the rush to appear youthful and "with it," so many adults have copied the teenagers' lifestyle that it is often not the adolescents who feel alienated from society (as they are supposed to) but their parents. Today, adolescents do set many trends, but their elevation to this role is a relatively recent phenomenon.

Before 1904 when G. Stanley Hall published his classic study, *Adolescence,* the word was not in common usage. People referred vaguely to "youth," a broad category consisting of older children and unmarried young adults, but they ascribed no special qualities to it. Then Hall, Erik Erikson, and other psychologists began to look more closely at what follows the onset of puberty. After analyzing the emotional upheavals of this period, especially the search for self-identity, they concluded that adolescence is a very distinct and critical stage of development unto itself.

It became even more distinct as secondary education mushroomed in the twentieth century. The high school did for teenagers what the elementary school had done for the younger children some two hundred years earlier in Europe: it removed them en masse from the mainstream of life and isolated them in an institution of their own. In time this institution fostered a specialized subculture. Adolescence now has its own standards, heroes, and, to a certain extent, its own language.

But even before the high school, children had had to grow from dependence to independence. And even before psychology told us why, children undergoing this metamorphosis had proved troublesome to themselves and to their world. Neither child nor adult, they didn't fit any identifiable niche. The males, particularly, seemed to threaten the established order. To control this age group and ease its growing pains, parents had resorted to a variety of tactics. Medieval noblemen had sent their children off to be pages at other castles, and many colonial farmers had bound their offspring out as apprentices. The elders of primitive societies, preferring a swifter, more concrete transition, often imposed gory tests of manhood. In the course of these puberty rites, a boy went from childhood to adulthood in his own eyes as well as those of his tribe—a very effective solution, indeed, to the "identity crisis." Among the ancients, Jews had initiated their sons into the adult community through a religious ceremony, the Bar Mitzvah, while Romans had marked the coming of age through an inscription in the roll of citizens.

In America rites of passage were never as dramatic or public as the rituals mentioned above. Since Americans conceived of growing up as a continuum, a progressive "lengthening of a person's shadow," there was no need to mark it off with ostentatious ceremonies. In the nineteenth century, for example, a girl usually "came out" in polite society merely by putting up her hair and letting down her skirts. Then, around World War I, girls stopped putting up their hair—they bobbed it. And the new society they helped create seemed anything but polite to their parents.

During the 1920s cars were introduced into American life on a mass-production basis. The automobile revolutionized adolescence by permitting teenagers to get away from adult supervision regularly and in private for the first time in history. The new "talkies" also broadened their horizons by introducing them to people and ideas they otherwise never would have known—and who their parents often didn't like one bit. On top of all this, sexual liberation was in the air. Sweet purity was no longer the most admired quality in a young lady; sex appeal was. The adolescent of the Roaring '20s tried to exude s.a. by hiking up her skirts, blacking her eyelids and rolling down her stockings. And it was in this guise, the getup of the flapper, that the modern teenager first appeared on the scene.

Many other guises were to follow, but in the next decade the teenager went into a temporary eclipse. This was the Great Depression of the 1930s and people had more on their minds than the wild ways of youth. Teenagers suffered hard times like everyone else and more than some, because employers often gave what little work there was to men with families. The lack of jobs combined with an extension of compulsory schooling to age sixteen, child labor laws, and the new minimum-wage acts kept more and more teenagers out of the labor market and in school. Automation reinforced this trend by eliminating many of the unskilled jobs traditionally filled by adolescents. And the new jobs being created were white collar positions, positions which required a high school diploma. For many reasons, then, secondary education eventually reached out to almost everyone in America between the ages of fourteen and eighteen. Whereas only 5 percent of the eighteen-year-olds were high school graduates in 1900, 75 percent were in 1975.

As the high school expanded, the look of the students continually changed. In the 1940s bobby-soxers wore plaid skirts and saddle shoes, in the 1950s their male counterparts had crew cuts and wore chinos with button-down shirts. Another element in the student body was considerably less clean-cut. These were the "greasers" who slicked back their long hair and wore pegged pants with black motorcycle jackets. By the end of the 1960s the diversity was gone; virtually all high school students, male and female, wore the same uniform of blue jeans, work shoes, and long hair.

But the change in adolescence in the '60s went far beyond fashion. Just as the 1920s separated the old-fashioned "youth" from the modern-day "teen," so the 1960s separated a conventionally moral type from a strikingly liberated one. Gone were the old associations of marriage and sex, love and sex, or, at the least, maturity and sex. Gone was the convenient double standard, and gone was the millennia-old ideal of female virginity before marriage.

Morals had been relaxing for some time, but the early and frequent sexual experiences of teenagers in the '60s marked a radical break with the past. No doubt the Pill, the new openness about sex, the glamorization of Playboy-style "fun" morality, and the breakdown of parental authority—or any authority—contributed to this revolution. But whatever its causes, it seems to be a revolution with staying power. And if society does not publicly condone teenage sex, at least it is no longer shocked by it. When former First Lady Betty Ford was asked how she would feel if her daughter, Susan, were having an affair, she replied, "I wouldn't be surprised. . . . She's a perfectly normal human being."

Sexual activity has its consequences—even in the 1970s—and teenagers apparently are not getting the information and contraceptive devices they need to minimize its risks. Venereal disease is rampant among adolescents today, while pregnancy is reaching epidemic proportions. Over a million adolescent girls became pregnant in 1975, many of them only fifteen years of age or younger. The Planned Parenthood Association of New York estimates that of the teenagers who became pregnant recently in that state, one-third had abortions, one-half gave birth out of wedlock, and the rest were married at the time of delivery. Young girls who go through with their pregnancies do so at high risk to their own health and that of their babies. Moreover, they may find that a society which condones illegitimacy among movie stars is often much harder on the unwed mother next door. Nor is the outlook very bright for the girls who marry young, because couples wed as teenagers have an extremely high rate of divorce.

The teenage subculture puts a great deal of pressure on youngsters to prove their sophistication by drinking to excess and experimenting with drugs as well as by "going all the way." But the adult world applies a great deal of pressure in its own way, too. Today, high school students are expected to make the team, make the prom, make grades, make college, make good. But make good in what direction? Our society offers an array of possibilities that is positively mind-boggling, and none of them—even the presidency of the United States—is considered too far above any individual.

In an isolated, static society, teenagers do not face this problem. They may enjoy a calm adolescence, secure in the knowledge that one day they will be just like their parents, doing what they do and believing what they believe. For them it is the only way. After contrasting teenage girls in remote villages in Samoa with our own youngsters, anthropologist Margaret Mead concluded that it is not the physiological changes of puberty but the need for decision-making that creates so much stress among American adolescents.

Recently, Dr. Mead commented on another aspect of adolescence, its increasing length. Pointing to such phenomena as the financially dependent graduate student and the very sophisticated preteen of eleven, she said we are witnessing a new trend. "In our time childhood has contracted," she claimed. "It is the years of adolescence that have stretched out." But though children may seem more grown-up today because of the way they dress and act, they are not in fact maturing any earlier. Children are taller and heavier today than in past centuries, but they are about the same size as their parents were at a comparable age. They are not reaching sexual maturity any earlier, either. Today, the average age at which a girl starts to menstruate is 12.8 years, the same point at which her mother physically came of age.

PARENTS: THEIR BACKS TO THE WALL

Two people who know they do not understand each other,

Breeding children whom they do not understand
And who will never understand them.
                              —T. S. Eliot, *The Cocktail Party*

Ever since people took notice of children, they have been formulating theories of how to rear them. For centuries most of these theories emphasized the children's duty to serve their parents and the parents' right to control their offspring. The control was to be maintained through fear. Then, with the advent of twentieth-century behaviorist psychology, it was to be maintained through training. Mixing old-fashioned Victorian notions and the latest scientific discoveries of conditioned responses, John B. Watson came up with a plan for child-rearing in which everything was to be done by the rules on a strict schedule. Watson discounted emotional needs and individual differences. For him nurture was everything—if you can call his austere regimen nurture:

> There is a sensible way of treating children. Treat them as though they were young adults. . . . Never hug and kiss them, never let them sit in your lap. . . . Give them a pat on the head if they have made an extraordinarily good job of a difficult task.

For every action in American child-rearing there is a reaction. "Permissiveness," which came into vogue as Watson's popularity declined, went to the opposite extreme in all but abolishing rules. Permissiveness was a child-centered approach. It was based on the Freudian theory that the less society blocked a child's desires, the better his chances were for becoming a happy, well-adjusted adult. Some extremists interpreted this to mean that the child, guided by his psychobiological drives, always knew his own needs best. The parental function was merely to help fulfill these needs. As permissiveness approached its peak in the decade following World War II, books appeared with such titles as *Stop Annoying Your Children* and *Parents, Behave!* But the book that came to stand for permissiveness was *The Common Sense Book of Baby and*

Child Care. It is the most widely read child care manual ever written, and its author, Benjamin Spock, is the most famous pediatrician who ever lived. Dr. Spock did believe in rules. However, he was so much more relaxed about them than the behaviorists that he seemed to be advocating permissiveness.

When the pendulum began to swing back, Dr. Spock and permissiveness were blamed for every problem parents had to face. During the 1960s those problems were numerous. Parents were presented with a totally new "scene": drugs, long hair, blue jeans, sit-ins, dropouts, hippies, and a sexual revolution. Children brought up to be neat were sloppy, those who were expected to succeed made sure to fail. Perhaps parents over-reacted to every change in lifestyle, perhaps children went out of their way to be perverse. Whatever the cause, the "generation gap" never seemed so wide. In retrospect some permissive parents blamed themselves for the way things turned out. As one of their number, Midge Decter, wrote in "A Letter to the Young":

> Believing you to be a new phenomenon among mankind— children raised exclusively on a principle of love, love unvaryingly acted out on our side and voluntarily offered on yours—we enthroned you as such. . . . [W]e refused to assume . . . one of the central obligations of parenthood: to make ourselves the final authority on good and bad, right and wrong, and to take the consequences of what might turn out to be a lifelong battle.

Many of the issues that divided parents and children in the 1960s have been resolved. But that doesn't mean that mothers and fathers now have an easier job of it. In fact, there are so many disruptive forces in American life today that, as Professor Urie Bronfenbrenner of Cornell has noted, it is "increasingly difficult for parents to behave as parents." Many fathers are either out of work or holding down two jobs to make ends meet. The widowed grandmother who used to keep an eye on the children now lives far away in an apartment of her own.

Families are constantly being uprooted, losing friends, status, and a sense of security in the process. And, more and more, they are suffering the trauma of divorce, which is ending one out of every two marriages in America today.

Our government has not been responsive to these problems. Although it spends billions to shore up faltering businesses, it is reluctant to spend a fraction of that amount to help shore up families. We say that families comprise the very foundation of our republic, yet we lag behind many industrialized nations in maternity arrangements, day-care institutions, and other social legislation. Why? Because despite their success elsewhere, cooperative child-rearing arrangements are suspect here, and even simple financial aid is frowned upon as "socialism." Mothers are supposed to raise their families in splendid isolation at home. But mothers are leaving home in droves. Over half of them already have jobs and the rate is increasing so rapidly that it has thrown every economic forecaster into confusion. It has also caught society unprepared with affordable, good child care. As a result, untold numbers of youngsters are "latchkey" children who must fend for themselves, often for several hours a day, until someone comes home.

Dr. Bronfenbrenner calls for family-support systems to help parents out. He claims that "A person cannot be committed to a child unless other people are committed to that person's commitment to children." Unfortunately, we don't have such systems and some parents simply cannot take the pressure of trying to go it alone. A baby's cries or an older child's back talk pushes them over the line and they lash out, beating the youngster with a hairbrush, throwing him against a wall, or thrusting his hand into a lit burner. Abuse is now the number two killer of children in America. But this may be only the tip of the iceberg because neglect, which is considered to be far more widespread than abuse, is hardly ever reported to the authorities. We don't know whether abuse is greater now than

ever before or whether recent publicity and nationwide reporting laws just make it seem so. We do know, however, that
widespread abuse and neglect mean that something is very
wrong in our society where children are concerned.

There are other indications of this as well. We have no room
in our economy for teenagers, for example, who have the
highest unemployment rate in the country. With nothing con-
structive to do, many of them get into trouble. Indeed, juvenile
delinquency is so prevalent in our society that statistically one
out of every nine youngsters will have to appear in court before
the age of eighteen. Children are running away from home at
the rate of a million a year, too. Although most of them don't go
far or stay long, some of them never return. And while the use
of hard drugs seems to be declining, alcoholism may be taking
its place among the young. Finally, emotional problems seem
to be on the rise, as indicated by a doubling of the teenage
suicide rate in the 1970s. Each year the number of children in
therapy goes up, but this may be more a function of society's
increasing psychological awareness rather than increasing mental disturbance.

Looking over this roster of ills, it is little wonder that parents
feel inadequate to the task of raising children in today's world.
T.V., movies, and peers seem to be vying with them for control
over their children's minds. Parents feel they lose the youngsters to these forces at an early age, but they don't know how
to get them back. They complain that "none of the old ways
prepare youth," but they don't know what new ways will,
either.

In an attempt to solve their dilemma, parents are frantically
reading advice books, calling TOT and Hot Lines, and forming
groups with names such as Parents Anonymous. Some fifty
thousand adults a year are also enrolling in psychologist
Thomas Gordon's Parent Effectiveness Training workshops to
learn the "no lose" method of child-rearing. But, unfortu-

nately, there are no magic formulas for familial harmony and no guarantees for a child's success. As Anne Roiphe, novelist and mother of five, has written:

> The dream of the young parent is that good parenting will produce a strong, kind, moral, successful, nearly perfect child, better than others, smarter than others, sensitive but no push-over—the ideal of a child reflecting and carrying on the good in the mother and father. The older parent fondly remembers those dreams so many compromises ago and is willing to settle for almost anything human at all.

To some people raising children just isn't worth the hassle and, in increasing numbers, they are choosing not to do it. This represents a radical change in American life because, until this time, the whole thrust of growing up was toward getting married and "settling down," i.e., having children. But today the emphasis is on personal fulfillment. Children, who used to be as sacrosanct as God, mother, country, and apple pie, are now deprecated for standing in the way of adult fun and, in the case of women, professional advancement. Although many people see "childless by choice" as a sensible adjustment to today's world, professor of philosophy Michael Novak, for one, takes a more cynical view of it:

> In our society, of course, there is no need to become an adult. One may remain—one is exhorted daily to remain—a child forever. . . . In medieval paintings, children look like miniature adults. In tableaux from life today, adults appear as wrinkled adolescents. . . . Children are not a welcome responsibility, for to have children is, plainly, to cease being a child oneself.

Childlessness by choice and other factors have sent the American birthrate plummeting. In the face of this, Professor Novak declares: "To choose to have a family used to be uninteresting. It is, today, an act of intelligence and courage."

Yet, despite later marriages, more divorces, the Pill, the Bomb, pollution, and the ecological appeal of Zero Population Growth, many people are still performing that act. In 1975 some 2.5 million Americans became parents for the first time and another 3.5 million increased their families. Today, there is no material value and little national good to be served by having children. But many parents still see it as the only way to get hold of the future, possess it, mold it, ensure it. For it is as true now as it was five thousand years ago that children represent the only immortality almost any of us will have.

CHAPTER NINE

CHILDHOOD:
THEN AND NOW

This is not a perfect world for children but, thanks to man-made progress, it is a far better world than they have ever known. Better nutrition and prenatal care have spectacularly increased the percentage of healthy, live births as have cleaner surroundings and new methods of handling premature and Rh-factor babies. Once only 50 percent or even less, the newborn's chances of surviving infancy in modern-day America are now 984.5 out of a thousand and in many countries they are even higher. Around the world infanticide has been replaced by new contraceptive and abortion techniques. In almost every country, too, children have benefited from more productive ways of farming, new methods of food preservation, and international cooperation. Today, they rarely suffer the devastating famines which claimed so many young lives through the ages. On a day-to-day basis, as well, they eat better and more regularly than ever before.

Children not only feel better as a result of their improved diet, but they are more resistant to disease, too. This resistance, combined with advances in medical science, no longer makes childhood one long series of illnesses. Smallpox has been wiped off the face of the earth. Other scourges of childhood such as polio, diphtheria, measles, mumps, whooping cough, tetanus, and German measles can now all be prevented through immunization. And many other formerly serious illnesses are treated so effectively with antibiotics that children are confined to their beds for only a day or two. Thanks to improved pediatric practices, bone fractures no longer cripple children for life and old-fashioned remedies such as bloodletting no longer kill while "curing" them. Ever since man learned how to purify water and pasteurize milk, children have been spared the infectious diseases carried by these often-polluted elements.

Children now enjoy a more pleasant existence as well as a healthier one. Because parents and teachers used to rely on fear in their dealings with children, beatings and other cruel punishments were a regular feature of childhood. A feminization of the child's world and a growing emphasis on humane treatment in society gradually led to a change in this approach. Spanking with a flexible palm on the buttocks replaced whipping with a rigid cane on the back, talking things out replaced locking a child up in a pitch-black cupboard. This change in disciplinary methods has been particularly dramatic in the classroom. Whereas the birch used to be *the* symbol of the pedagogue, corporal punishment is now a rare occurrence. Some people would like to see it abolished altogether, but the Supreme Court has been reluctant to do so. However, the Court did recently put curbs on the practice, saying that clear warnings must be issued ahead of time; other means of control must be tried first; and then, if a teacher does proceed, she may not strike a child with "unreasonable force."

The humane movement has been of particular benefit to illegitimate children. Throughout the ages they were the chief victims of infanticide, and even when they were allowed to live, they were granted little familial protection and few legal rights. They were the outcasts of society. Today few children suffer as they once did from the appellation "bastard." Indeed, as the practice of adoption has grown and the supply of available babies has shrunk, many families now pay upward of five thousand dollars for the white babies who are at a premium. Adoptees have the same social standing and legal rights as anyone else in America. And even illegitimate children who are not legally adopted now enjoy firmer claims to their parents' estates than ever before.

Orphans have also benefited from society's deepening compassion. Communities once discharged their duty to orphans by binding them out as servants or incarcerating them in workhouses. Later they built orphanages for them. Although these were an improvement over earlier arrangements, orphanages were still cold places. Today, the orphanage has all but vanished from America, thanks to the fact that parents are living longer. In cases where both parents have died, their children are usually taken in by relatives or put up for adoption. "Social orphans," those whose parents cannot or will not take care of them, are placed in foster homes. There is much in foster care to criticize, principally its lack of permanence, but it is still a vast improvement over the cold, impersonal treatment which used to be meted out to homeless children.

Society used to exact its due not only from the orphan, but also from the poor child. He, too, was bound into servitude and he, too, was thrown into the workhouse. Then the feeling began to take hold that the state's proper function was to help poor children, not punish them, and, as government gained ever greater powers, it did just that. Its first affirmative action was the establishment of minimum-age laws which did away with child labor, that scourge of the poor. Today, millions of children receive food, clothing, shelter, and medical attention through the largesse of the United States government. Some people object to our government giving out these welfare benefits and others say it is not doing enough. But welfare has provided a floor, at least, under human misery, for while many children are undernourished in modern-day America, they do not starve.

Since World War II the federal government has gone beyond the limited goals of welfare in an attempt to extend the American Dream to underprivileged children. Typically, it has pinned its hopes on education to bring black and white, rich and poor together. First the government desegregated the schools, then it turned its attention to the classroom experience itself. Since 1965 it has allocated over one billion dollars a year to meet "the special educational needs of disadvantaged children." A great deal of this money has gone for general school use, but some of it has been used to fund new compensatory education programs, such as Head Start and Operation Follow-Through.

The most recent major movement to affect children in our society is Women's Liberation. Although the position of women in our society has slowly been changing, the assumptions governing girlhood—and boyhood—have not. We still believe that girls and boys are inherently and importantly different. Boys are supposed to be active, tough, adventurous, mischievous. Girls should be passive, soft, domestic, gentle, loving, and, above all, pretty. Boys are the resourceful, courageous leaders; girls the silly, fearful followers.

In the past boys fulfilled their promise by becoming the economic providers. Girls fulfilled theirs by becoming wives and mothers. Poor women have always worked, of course, and some middle-class women even had careers, but the latter group usually consisted of those who had "unfortunately" lost their chance at marriage. Moreover, the careers open to them were generally as "helpers": teachers, nurses, social workers. Few girls were encouraged to try a higher profession and, when a bold one did, she often found her path blocked by its male practitioners. Over time the feeling grew that girls should have more education, but this was only to make them more desirable mates, more intelligent mothers, and more cultured tastemakers. Thus, although the number of female college graduates rose dramatically in the twentieth century, the proportion of female doctors, dentists, and lawyers held steady at well under 10 percent of the total number of practitioners.

Feminists are out to change all that. They are demanding equal employment opportunities for women, equal pay for equal work, and affirmative-action programs in professional schools as well as in industry. They are also calling upon men to take over more of the "women's work" at home. As part of the new order, they are trying to create a new child, one who will not be hampered by the stereotypes of the past. Thus, mothers who have had their consciousness raised are giving fire trucks to their daughters and baby dolls to their sons. They are reading both sexes stories in which the girls get to build the tree house, for once, and mothers do more than set out milk and cookies. Ironically, their efforts may do more to "liberate" their sons than their daughters, for while it has been considered cute for some time for a girl in our society to be a tomboy, it is still frowned upon for a boy to be a "sissy."

Today, in their heart-to-heart talks, mothers are telling daughters that they are just as important as their brothers. They are also saying that catching a husband is not the only or even the most worthwhile goal in life, that a girl should reach as high as any boy in America, maybe all the way up to President of the United States. This advice represents a radical break with the past. But it suits the present and, even more importantly, it suits the future because women are entering the job market by the millions. And, if future trends continue, they will not be content with the low-paying, low-status jobs that have been their lot in the past.

Not a movement but an object, television, may turn out to make the greatest changes of all in childhood. Of course, children have always had their amusements and an enormous assortment of dolls, balls, hoops, board games and pull toys it has been. But there is one great difference between these traditional amusements and television: with the former, children actively participated; with the latter, they passively observe. Moreover, unlike any other toy in history, television now absorbs more of a youngster's time than school, games, or any other activity except sleep.

As with permissive upbringing, T.V. has been blamed for every ill besetting the younger generation from falling test scores to juvenile delinquency. Some studies indicate that watching violence on T.V. makes children more tolerant of violence. Yet whether they will grow up to become violent people as a result, we do not know. We are also not sure if their new ability to be entertained by merely flicking a dial makes children lazier, less prone to read, or less tolerant of frustration, as critics claim. And we may never know. There are too many factors operating in our society to isolate direct cause-and-effect relationships. Moreover, since 95 percent of the households in America have T.V. sets, it is very difficult to find nonwatchers to compare with the watchers. On the positive side, though, television seems to be giving young children a more extensive vocabulary and a greater awareness of the world than they otherwise would have. It is also creating a common cultural background for youngsters much as the *McGuffey Readers* did a hundred years earlier. Along with mandatory education, television is making childhood a more uniform experience than ever before.

Just as we do not know what will be the ultimate impact of T.V., so we cannot predict what will come of other recent developments in our society. Not so long ago the average child had three siblings. Today, statistically, he has less than one. Not so long ago children spent six years in school; today they spend thirteen years there or more. And not so long ago children were inevitabilities; now their births can be prevented at will. Today we are seeing a phenomenal increase in broken homes, working mothers, traveling fathers, too much sugar, and not enough fiber in the diet. What will it all add up to? Theories abound, but in fact we are too close to these phenomena to correctly assess them. Only time will reveal their true impact on childhood in America.

NEW GODS FOR THE SPACE AGE?

Throughout the ages children were valued for the contribution they made to the family economy. And in most societies around the world today, children are still expected to do a substantial portion of the work. Young children fetch and carry small parcels, run errands, and bear messages. In agricultural societies older children weed and hoe, fish, trap small animals, tend the barnyard flock, and carry loads of produce from the fields. In socialist countries it is often the state not the family to which children contribute, but contribute they do and from a very early age. Thus, in the Soviet Union four- and five-year-olds clear a snowy path to their own nursery school, and in China tots of the same age fold boxes which will hold crayons for export.

Around the world children are the principal baby-sitters, taking charge of younger siblings so that their mothers can tend to other tasks. Although most sitters are at least seven, in the Philippines some children are trained from the age of three to rock the baby, and in other places five-year-olds attend kindergarten with infants strapped to their backs. Whether sweeping out the house, tending a state-run children's farm, or watching their younger sisters and brothers, children do meaningful, necessary work a part of each day everywhere in the world—everywhere, that is, except in America.

American society asks for and gets a bare minimum from its children. This phenomenon stems from our reliance on mechanical aids, our traditional use of paid helpers, a long school day, strict child labor laws, and the complex nature of our civilization. But mostly it stems from our image of childhood as a time of "fun." Anthropologists Beatrice and John Whiting, among others, feel that we are not doing our children any favors with this attitude. In their book *Children of Six Cultures,* the Whitings concluded that children whose work has a direct bearing on the life of the group have a greater sense of self-worth than our own youngsters, whose household and school tasks seem to be make-work. Moreover, the Whitings found that children in simple cultures who are full-time baby-sitters are more nurturant and responsible than their American counterparts.

But are they any happier? This is the first question that would spring from the lips of many American parents, to whom happiness is the single criterion of a good childhood. The happy childhood was invented by the Romantic writers in the late eighteenth century. Since then we have had almost no direct testimony from children to prove or disprove its existence, and it is quite possible that childhood may be truly happy only in retrospect when one has a burdened adulthood to compare it to. Yet, though the happy childhood may be an impossible dream, many American parents are trying to make it come true for their offspring. More and more adults have the money to shower gifts upon their children and the leisure time to drum up new ways of making them happy. But, according to psychiatrist Robert Coles, their efforts may be having the opposite effect. Nowadays children are forced to cope with an avalanche of possessions and possibilities which they are not equipped to handle.

The modern-day practice of gifting children bears a strange resemblance to the sacrifices once made upon the altars of heathen gods. And, in our increasingly secular age, it does seem that children have become the central figures of a new suburban theology. Its credo is summarized this way by Robert Coles: "I don't believe in an afterlife. I don't believe in God. What I really believe in is my children. I'm going to give them the best of everything." Unfortunately, as Dr. Coles points out, "That kind of faith generates demands on these children such as no other generation has ever had to face."

SELECTED BIBLIOGRAPHY

Ariès, Philippe. *Centuries of Childhood*. N.Y.: Random House, 1960.

Bett, Henry. *The Games of Children:* Their Origin and History. Detroit: Singing Tree Press, 1968.

Bettelheim, Bruno. *The Children of the Dream*. N.Y.: The Macmillan Company, 1969. Communal child-rearing in Israel.

————. *The Uses of Enchantment*. The Meaning and Importance of Fairy Tales. N.Y.: Alfred A. Knopf, 1977.

Boas, George. *The Cult of Childhood*. London: University of London, 1966.

Bremner, Robert, ed. et al. *Children and Youth in America:* A Documentary History. 3 vols. Cambridge, Mass.: Harvard University Press, 1970–74.

Bronfenbrenner, Urie. *Two Worlds of Childhood: U.S. and U.S.S.R.* N.Y.: Basic Books, 1970.

Coveney, Peter. *The Image of Childhood*. Baltimore: Penguin Books, 1967.

de la Mare, Walter. *Early One Morning in the Spring*. London: Faber & Faber, 1935. Memoirs and other writings about childhood.

deMause, Lloyd, ed. *The History of Childhood*. N.Y.: The Psychohistory Press, 1974.

Demos, John. *A Little Commonwealth:* Family Life in Plymouth Colony. N.Y.: Oxford University Press, 1970.

Earle, Alice Morse. *Child Life in Colonial Days*. N.Y.: The Macmillan Company 1899.

Erikson, Erik H. *Childhood and Society*. N.Y.: W. W. Norton & Co., 1950.

Fraser, Antonia. *A History of Toys*. London: George Weidenfeld & Nicolson, 1966.

Garland, Madge. *The Changing Face of Childhood*. London: Hutchinson & Co., 1963. The child in art.

Goldstein, Joseph; Freud, Anna; and Solnit, Albert J. *Beyond the Best Interests of the Child*. N.Y.: The Free Press, 1973. Child placement by the courts.

Handlin, Oscar and Handlin, Mary F. *Facing Life:* Youth and the Family in American History. Boston: Little, Brown and Co., 1971.

Hechinger, Fred M. and Hechinger, Grace. *Growing Up in America*. N.Y.: McGraw-Hill, 1975. A history of education.

Helfer, Ray E. and Kempe, C. Henry. *The Battered Child*. Chicago: University of Chicago Press, 1968.

Holt, John. *Escape from Childhood*. N.Y.: E. P. Dutton & Co., 1974. A radical view of children's rights.

Hürlimann, Bettina. *Three Centuries of Children's Books in Europe*. Cleveland: World Publishing Co., 1967.

Journal of Psychohistory (History of Childhood Quarterly). Summer, 1973 vol. I, no. 1 and all volumes following.

Kessen, William. *The Child*. N.Y.: John Wiley & Sons, Inc., 1965. Writings in child psychology from 1693.

Lacey, W. K. *The Family in Classical Greece*. Ithaca, N.Y.: Cornell University Press, 1968.

Lasareff, Victor. "Studies in the Iconography of the Virgin." *Art Bulletin* 20 (1938): pp. 26–65. Changing image of the Christ Child in art.

Liebert, Robert M.; Neale, John M.; and Davidson, Emily S. *The Early Window:* Effects of Television on Children and Youth. N.Y.: Pergamon Press, Inc., 1973.

Marrou, H. I. *A History of Education in Antiquity*. N.Y.: Sheed and Ward, 1956.

McClinton, Katharine Morrison. *Antiques of American Childhood*. N.Y.: Bramhall House, 1970.

McGraw, Myrtle. *The Child in Painting*. N.Y.: The Greystone Press, 1941.

Mead, Margaret. *Coming of Age in Samoa*. N.Y.: William Morrow, 1928.

———. *Culture and Commitment*. A Study of the Generation Gap. N.Y.: The Natural History Press, 1970.

——— and Calas, Nicolas, eds. *Primitive Heritage*. N.Y.: Random House, 1953.

——— and Wolfenstein, Martha, eds. *Childhood in Contemporary Cultures*. Chicago: University of Chicago Press, 1955.

Meigs, Cornelia ed. et al. *A Critical History of Children's Literature.* N.Y.: The Macmillan Company, 1969.

Miller, Nathan. *The Child in Primitive Society.* N.Y.: Brentano's, 1928.

Morgan, Edmund S. *The Puritan Family:* Religion and Domestic Relations in Seventeenth Century New England. N.Y.: Harper & Row, 1966.

Opie, Iona and Opie, Peter. *The Oxford Book of Children's Verses.* N.Y.: Oxford University Press, 1973.

Payne, George Henry. *The Child in Human Progress.* N.Y.: G. P. Putnam's Sons, 1916.

Pinchbeck, Ivy and Hewitt, Margaret. *Children in English Society.* 2 vols. Toronto: University of Toronto Press, 1969–1973.

The Rights of Children. Reprint Series No. 9. Cambridge, Mass.: Harvard Educational Review, 1974.

Ritchie, Oscar W. and Koller, Marvin R. *Sociology of Childhood.* N.Y.: Appleton-Century-Crofts, 1964.

Rousseau, Jean Jacques. *Émile.* N.Y.: E. P. Dutton, 1969.

Ruhräh, John. *Pediatrics of the Past.* N.Y.: Paul B. Hoeber, Inc., 1925.

Segal, Julius and Yahraes, Herbert. *A Child's Journey:* Forces that Shape the Lives of Our Young. N.Y.: McGraw-Hill, 1978.

Sidel, Ruth. *Women and Child Care in China.* N.Y.: Hill and Wang, 1972.

Still, George F. *The History of Paediatrics.* London: Oxford University Press, 1931.

Sussman, Alan. *The Rights of Young People.* N.Y.: Avon Books, 1977.

Washington, Booker T. *Up From Slavery.* N.Y.: Dell Publishing Co., 1965.

Whiting, Beatrice and Whiting, John. *Children of Six Cultures.* Cambridge, Mass.: Harvard University Press, 1975.

Wickes, Ian G. "A History of Infant Feeding." *Archives of Disease in Childhood* 28 (1953): April, June, Aug., Oct., Dec.

Wishy, Bernard W. *The Child and the Republic:* The Dawn of Modern American Child Nurture. Philadelphia: University of Pennsylvania Press, 1968.

INDEX